Southern Discomfort

Does the Land of the Eternal Sauna leave you hot under the collar?

Is your temperature boiling now that termites, roaches, ants and mosquitoes have become permanent houseguests?

Do you lie awake under your jet-propelled ceiling fan, fuming about the horrendous heat and humidity?

Well chill out!

Don't sweat it!

Laugh with Debby Wood as she blows off steam about the burning issues of life in fabulous Florida. You'll find her breezy style and irreverent humor a breath of fresh air and a marvelous remedy for your southern discomfort.

Also by Debby Wood:

"Oh, God, Not Another Beautiful Day!"
Middle age and other spreads
FLORIDA: A Slice of Paradise

Copyright 1991 by Debby Wood

Library of Congress Catalog Number: 91-92889

International Standard Book Number: 0-9607490-2-0

Printed and bound in the United States of America
BookCrafters, Inc.

Debby Wood

Confessions Of A Frazzled Floridian

You don't have to be born in Florida to be a native. With about a thousand people moving to the Sunshine State every day, this place is growing so fast that if you've been around for more than five years your friends and neighbors start asking you what it was like back in the "old days."

I've been living in Florida for well over a decade. That makes me what they call a "semi-native."

When my neighbors ask what Florida was like when I first arrived, I tell them it was more or less the same ... more fish, less cars, more seashells, less banks.

Today I feel like a pioneer. Back then I felt like an unwilling participant in some sort of giant science project gone awry.

I stepped off the plane in July, 1977, and was nearly knocked over by the humidity. My beautifully combed hair immediately turned to frizz.

The drip-dry blouse I was wearing started to drizzle. My first purchase was industrial-strength deodorant.

I went house hunting and could concentrate on nothing but the dead roaches I saw in every closet. Each time I stepped from the car I was attacked by some invisible form of wildlife the Realtor referred to as "no-see-ums."

"There's no way I'm moving down there," I told my husband after our first trip to Florida. "I have no desire to coexist with alligators, mosquitoes or mold. And I'm too young to live with continual hot flashes."

My husband, however, was euphoric. He had finally found paradise.

"Just give it three years," he pleaded. "If you don't like it after three years, we'll move back north."

What a joke! The only way I could get him to leave his little slice of paradise is if a hurricane picked him up and deposited him somewhere north of the Mason-Dixon line.

During that first year in Florida it seemed like my husband and I were looking at different worlds.

He saw lush tropical vegetation, spectacular sunsets, and white, sandy beaches. I saw bugs, sand burs, and what looked like utility poles with green leaves sprouting out of the top, which the natives called "trees."

He would go outside and soak up the rays of sun. I would huddle inside under the air conditioner.

During the second year I devoted most of my energy to battling mildew and trying to outwit the kamikaze mosquitoes, so anxious to bite that they were willing to die for the chance.

In my third year our family bought a boat and discovered a whole new Florida. I learned how to catch catfish. I found that a boat without a bilge pump is likely to become a submarine. And I discovered boats don't come equipped with brakes.

During the fourth year I stopped screaming every time I saw a roach. That was also the year I started referring to roaches as "palmetto bugs," especially in front of northern visitors.

By year five I realized I was going to serve a life sentence in Florida. I held a huge garage sale and got rid of all my wool clothes, snow shovels, and other crutches I'd been holding on to in hopes of returning "home." It was a turning point.

I made it through the entire summer of my sixth year before I realized I hadn't purchased the mandatory candles, batteries, canned food and water in preparation for the hurricanes that never came. I hadn't even taped a tracking map to the refrigerator door.

In the seventh year I discovered I'd been wearing flipflops so long, I couldn't squeeze my feet into any of my shoes. When I bought a new pair of shoes, I had to increase two sizes!

By the eighth year my dreams of experiencing a "white" Christmas were little more than a memory. I no longer suffered pangs of guilt while explaining to my kids that Santa arrives in a helicopter. Twinkle lights wrapped around cactus plants started to look festive rather than tacky.

At some point during my ninth year I found myself eating soggy crackers without complaining. I heard myself tell a house guest, "Hey, what's a little mold as long as it's in the closet instead of on the food."

In year ten we sold the boat. It was a traumatic moment because I could no longer enjoy the water. It was also traumatic for our boat repairman, who had to find some other sucker to pay for those European vacations he enjoyed every year.

After eleven years of battling love bugs, I impulsively sprayed Pam on the hood of my car one day, hoping the little creatures would slide off like a strip of bacon leaving a frying pan. Unfortunately, the brutal Florida sun baked the Pam on my car before the love bugs had a chance to slide off. Now you really can fry an egg on my car.

During my twelfth year I became more conscious of the environment. I wouldn't allow any family member outside without a two-inch-thick layer of sunscreen covering all exposed body parts. Trips to the beach were off limits. And any house guest wanting to sit outside at night had to sign a form releasing me from any responsibility in case they were bitten by an encephalitis-bearing mosquito.

Midway through my second decade in paradise, I can wave good-bye to one carload of house guests at noon, strip the guest room bed, clean the house, and greet the next carload of house guests by 3 in the afternoon.

I know how to take the sting out of a jelly fish wound, how to remove a sand bur from a bare foot, and how to protect my skin from "no-see-ums."

I know just when to pass another car on the right, which restaurants have the best salad bars, and where to go to see an alligator.

I spend my days in hair curlers, and my nights in hair curlers.

I look at palmetto bugs as constant house guests, not at all bashful about joining you at the dinner table.

I realize that it's a battlefield outside, and that we're losing the war. Someday the bugs will circle around our inert bodies, and the frogs and lizards will go in for the kill.

It no longer bothers me that we're living on land roughly one foot above sea level, and that the slightest bit of rain will turn my yard into a swamp.

But every once in a while I find myself longing to see some daffodils, or a maple tree getting ready for winter.

"Remember your promise to move back north if I didn't like Florida after three years?" I asked my husband one day.

"What on earth are you talking about?" he said. "Are you crazy? I'd never make a deal like that!"

The rest, as they say, is history. I've learned to tolerate the place, hot flashes and all. And who knows, in another decade I may actually start to like Florida. Then again ...

Some Like It Hot

Out of every 1,000 couples in Florida, there is probably one husband and wife team that doesn't fight over the thermostat. At least I'd like to think so.

Nearly everyone I talk to has a spouse who can't stand the heat ... or the cold.

When we moved to Florida, it didn't take long for me to realize that our marriage was on tenuous ground. My husband thrives on the heat. I long for the cold.

As the movers unpacked the boxes in the living room, I stood there in the unspeakable Florida heat, gasping for oxygen, asking myself, "How could this have happened?"

Beads of sweat dangled from the tip of my nose. My clothes smelled like I just stepped out of a high school locker room. I was near hysteria.

"Can't we turn on the air conditioner for just a little

bit?" I asked my husband.

"Don't be ridiculous," he said. "All the doors are wide open. The movers are walking in and out of the house. Why should we try to cool off the entire neighborhood?"

It went on and on like this. I claimed he didn't love me. He claimed I didn't know the value of a dollar. I accused him of being a Scrooge. He made obscene hand gestures. I threatened to leave. He dared me. The movers had quite a show!

It was one of those hot moments that you read about in the newspaper where they quote the neighbors as saying, "I knew she was upset, but I never dreamed she was the kind of woman who would stab her husband to death with a corkscrew."

That was our first argument in what has become a long war over the thermostat. It was also the moment I realized that Florida, contrary to all those travel brochures, is not really heaven on earth.

"People weren't really meant to live in Florida during the summer months," my neighbor told me as she closed up her house and returned north in May. It only took me one experience with a broken air conditioner in July to understand the reality of that statement.

I pride myself on being able to roll with the punches. I can overcome adversity and laugh in the face of danger. I don't let hardship get me down.

But I can't live without air conditioning. It gives new meaning to the word "despair."

The cold air stopped coming through the little ceiling vents at 7:30 on one of the muggiest nights of the year.

By 7:45 p.m. I was hysterical, running through the house opening all the windows.

By 8:10 I had eaten an entire gallon of ice cream.

10

By 8:35 I was irrational. I started putting packages of frozen food in every room to cool the house.

By 9:05 I was packing up and heading for the nearest motel.

I never thought of myself as a wimp, but the frightening realization that my air conditioner might be added to the endangered species list reduced me to tears.

I don't take much in life for granted, but I've always had a firm conviction that man has an unalienable right to free speech, liberty, and cool air. And not necessarily in that order.

After all, we know what it took to turn Florida from a swamp into paradise — air conditioning. Before central air came along, the sunshine state was merely a sleepy appendage to the rest of the country. Air conditioning made the south nearly liveable. It also made a lot of real estate people very rich.

During June, July and August, this place is like a jungle. Fungus forms on your skin, in your shoes, on your furniture and in your car.

You open your front door and you feel as though a giant Saint Bernard dog is breathing on you. All that is missing is the slobber dripping from his mouth.

The heat is so intense that lawns turn brown in an afternoon. Certain things thrive in such an atmosphere: mildew, fleas, sand burs, mold, red ants, hurricanes, hot tempers and sunburn.

Is it any wonder why people close their windows and doors in the summer and turn down the thermostat? So what if you have to pay electric bills the size of the federal deficit.

Who can put a price tag on paradise?

R-V Having Fun Yet?

I have a recurring nightmare.

It begins with a horn blaring somewhere in the distance. I open the front door and all I can see is fog.

Suddenly, out of the mist, my husband appears, driving a 40-foot-long recreational vehicle. He parks the camper in the driveway, climbs out, and with a smile a mile wide says, "Surprise! Look what I bought!"

12

That's when I wake up and start pounding him with my pillow.

I don't know why I've been having this nightmare so often. It must have something to do with my friend Nelda, who just spent four weeks touring the Northeast in a Winnebago with three preteen boys, a dog in heat, and a husband who yearned for the open road.

"Why did you do it?" I asked as she threw the seventh load of dirty laundry into her washing machine on the morning after her return.

"What else could I do?" she said in exasperation. "This was Harold's lifelong dream. I just didn't have the heart to say no."

"Was it as bad as you thought?" I asked.

"Worse! You just cannot imagine!"

She led me out to the camper and pushed me inside.

"That's where I slept," she said, pointing to what looked like a padded park bench. "Every time I turned over in my sleep, I would fall onto the floor."

She couldn't sleep in the bunk beds, she explained, because they were so close to the ceiling that there wasn't enough room for her to climb in. Therefore the kids got the choice sleeping accommodations.

"What did you do for four weeks?" I asked.

"Harold drove, the kids fought, and I cried," she said. "I also washed a lot of dishes."

"But what about the marshmallow roasts, the serenity, the great outdoors?"

"Those are just come-ons that someone in an advertising agency dreamed up," she said. "And the men naturally believe them."

For Harold, camping means picnicking under a shady oak tree beside a breezy lake, savoring a peaceful walk on a tree-lined trail, and singing around a blazing camp-fire beneath starry skies.

For Nelda, camping means trying to open a can of beans with a screwdriver without severing any fingers, never having quite enough bug spray, and washing yourself in a shower stall that isn't big enough to turn around in.

"During the third week I seriously contemplated divorce," she said. "But Harold kept assuring me that things would get better. I now realize he was lying through his teeth."

It rained most of the fourth week.

"Every time the kids went outside, they would slip and fall in the mud. One night their shoes were so dirty I just threw them in the trash can and we drove away."

As we walked away from the camper, I noticed a "FOR SALE" sign on the front window.

"Either that thing goes or I go," Nelda said.

"Was Harold upset when you told him?"

"No. He's got his eye on a sailboat. He thinks it would be fun for all of us to sail to the Bahamas next summer."

Some people never learn!

The Car Wars State

Anyone who has spent a winter in Florida shouldn't really be surprised to hear the news that this state now has more cars than people.

Florida highway researchers figure the state has about

12 vehicles for every 10 people. That makes us one mobile society!

Of course if you've ever been stuck in the gridlock caused by a few drops of rain, you already knew that. You're also aware of the motor madness that results from so many vehicles on the road.

Part of the culture shock everyone faces after moving to Florida is learning to cope with so many crazy drivers.

There's **Mr. Nice Guy**, who is never in a hurry and will bring traffic to a halt at the very sight of a little old lady crossing a street three blocks away.

Mr. Nice Guy will wait at a stop sign for 20 minutes letting traffic from every side of the street pass, completely oblivious to the line of cars behind him that stretches almost to the Georgia border.

He may spend five minutes rolling down his window so he can hear what all the other motorists are shouting at him. Hopefully, his hearing aid won't pick up every single word!

Mr. Nice Guy drives **Defiant Driver** crazy! Defiant treats every hour of the day as rush hour. He's always in more of a hurry than the drivers around him.

Defiant whips out of his driveway in the morning, never quite stops at those silly red octagonal signs, and treats every yellow traffic signal as a personal challenge.

You can spot Defiant going to the limit in every driving situation. He's the last one to merge, even in the face of oncoming traffic. He's the first one out of the toll booth. He can wedge his car into a five-foot hole at the head of any line of waiting traffic.

Often there is a passenger riding in Defiant's car, clutching the dashboard and hyperventilating in tight situations.

The **Primper** never sees Defiant's close calls. That's because the Primper is always looking in the rear-view mirror, checking to make sure every strand of hair is in place.

Male Primpers shave, comb their mustaches, and straighten their ties, all while traveling along at 60 miles-per-hour.

Female Primpers remove their hair curlers, apply lipstick, eye shadow and mascara, and floss their teeth so they'll look decent when they step out of their car or arrive at work.

Primpers cause **Neurotic Drivers** to honk their horns in frustration. Of course frustration is a way of life for the Neurotic Driver.

He lurks around the supermarket parking lot, dodging past stray shopping carts in an effort to get the prized parking spot in front of the store.

He shouts at jaywalkers, curses potholes, and makes hand gestures at anyone or anything in his way. And he's always in a hurry because he has five minutes to get to an important meeting 30 miles away.

I tell you, it's like Car Wars out there. No wonder there are so many extra vehicles in Florida. We need the spare parts!

A Place For Everything, And Nothing In Its Place

Does the floor of your bedroom closet look like the Imelda Marcos Memorial Shoe Collection?

Are you having trouble finding your toaster because your kitchen counter is covered with so much clutter?

Is your garage so full of junk that the only vehicle there's room for is your child's scooter?

Then it's time for that favorite ritual ... **spring cleaning!**

Listen up, all you messies. Come out of the closet (if you can open the door) and get organized.

You know who you are.

You're the one who's been stashing all those used plastic margarine containers for the past 10 years just in case your child might need them for a Scout seedling project. Toss them! Your child is about to graduate from college.

You're the one who searches the house for postage stamps and finds only the eight-cent variety. Get with the times! Those stamps went out of style years ago.

You're the one who looks at those closet organizer systems and thinks, "Maybe that would solve my problem." Get real!

I know who you are because I'm one of you.

In our house, everything has its place, but nothing's in it. The car keys are never in my purse. They're in the kitchen drawer, or behind the bread box, or in the toy chest.

The scissors are never in the kitchen drawer. They're

on the bathroom counter, or in the toy chest, or wedged between the sofa pillows.

Incoming mail is lucky to make it past the garage door, something that bill collectors just don't seem to understand.

I've got a junk drawer stuffed full of things like stray rubber bands, old Christmas cards, rusty paper clips, dried-out ball-point pens, my 19-year-old daughter's first grade report card, broken rulers, assorted coins, a swimmer's nose clip, a few playing cards, and a fondue fork that is forever getting wedged in such a way as to make it impossible to open the drawer.

The floor of my closet is covered with stray shoulder pads, hole-ridden pantyhose, and clothes that have been waiting for the ironing board for the past four years.

In my dresser are gifts I can't use and can't return (and don't have the nerve to give to someone else). Like the handmade sweater with shoulders that would fit King Kong, or the "I Love Cleveland" ashtray, or the set of purple monogrammed bath towels.

My hall closet is full of items that haven't seen the light of day since Nehru jackets were in style. There's a Flying Nun Halloween costume. Several unhung pictures that would look great in a cheap motel room. A complete assortment of attachments to the vacuum cleaner we gave to the Goodwill in 1984. A cracked fish bowl full of unmarked keys. And a selection of games, from Candyland to Twister.

But the most visible sign of my lack of organization is the pile of stuff (and I use the word loosely) on my kitchen counter. Everyone knows not to interfere with my "pile." It contains important notes ... notes so cryptic that when I read them, I can't imagine what I was trying

to tell myself.

There are slips of paper containing phone numbers, but I have no idea who the numbers belong to, and I'm too embarrassed to dial them and ask, "Who is this?" There are faded newspaper clippings, grease-stained recipes, expired coupons, unpaid bills, credit card charge slips, tiny packages of ketchup from fast-food restaurants, product warranties, snapshots from our 1986 vacation, and assorted homework assignments.

Each year my husband sorts through my pile for receipts that may come in handy for our tax return. And each year he grumbles about my lack of organization.

"So what if a doctor's bill got stuck in my recipe file by accident," I told him last April as he tore through my kitchen hunting for receipts. "I was making croissants after I got home from the doctor, and I must have put the bill back in the file instead of the recipe. I would have found it sooner or later."

He pulled a gasoline sales slip out of the silverware drawer, looked at me with a scowl, and told me I had to become more organized.

He doesn't realize that it could be worse.

My friend Nelda keeps a similar pile near her kitchen phone. Last month she took the whole pile and stuck it in her oven because she was having a party and wanted her house to look neat and organized.

I was driving past her house a few days later and saw a fire truck parked out front. Nelda was standing by the front door, clearly humiliated.

"I forgot about the pile of papers I stashed in my oven," she told me. "This morning I turned the oven on and everything caught fire."

I guess that's one way to start your spring cleaning!

Our Cold-Weather Clothes Have Lost Their Cool

On those rare occasions when the thermometer dips below 50 degrees, Florida starts looking like a walking thrift shop.

Long-time residents dig out winter clothes they haven't worn since the early 1960s, and nothing matches.

Along comes a cold front and retired auto executives normally at home on a golf course start dressing like derelicts in clothing that should have been sold at a garage sale.

Let the temperature drop to 40 degrees and women who are perfectly comfortable hosting cocktail parties at the country club don outfits that make them resemble bag ladies from New York City.

During a two-day cold snap last winter, my husband and I went to the local supermarket to pick up a few cans of soup. When we got inside, I thought we had entered a soup kitchen in the Bowery.

Most of the shoppers were dressed in shabby old parkas or moth-eaten coats, looking like they had just spent the night sleeping on the sidewalk.

"I guess we're only about 10 degrees away from looking like characters in a movie about the Great Depression," my husband observed.

He was looking at a woman wearing a bright blue maxi-coat right out of the '60s. It covered everything but her purple fur-lined boots and her green holey mittens.

"That's for sure," I said, pointing to an elderly man dressed in a faded wool pea coat, the lining of which was hanging from the lower hem. The top of the coat was held together with a big safety pin, and the scarf around his neck looked like it had been jammed into a pocket for at least two decades.

The man was with a woman wearing a red wool coat with a fur collar that I swear could have come out of my grandmother's closet in 1955.

"I've seen panhandlers with more class!"

It's easy to spot the recent arrivals to Florida. They're decked out in matching parkas or fashionable ski outfits, ready to brave the near-freezing temperatures.

But for the rest of us who haven't had to shop for winter clothes since we left the North, dressing for cold weather requires special effort.

When my husband and I took the kids to the mountains one Thanksgiving, it was the first time we had been in cold weather for nine years.

I spent weeks borrowing winter coats, long under-wear, scarfs, mittens, and hats from all my friends and neighbors so we would be prepared for the worst.

Luckily, we hit snow and had a chance to ski. We looked like a family of refugees, skiing down the mountain in a rag-tag assortment of mismatched clothing. People talked to us slowly, enunciating every syllable, assuming we were just off the boat.

Back in Florida, however, we're right at home.

I looked at my husband as he was paying the supermarket cashier for the soup. He was wearing faded corduroy bell-bottom trousers, a wool plaid shirt and contrasting plaid scarf, underneath a coat that had seen better days.

And I was dressed in my old fake fur coat that smells like moth balls and resembles the skin of a wet yak.

Maybe we've been in Florida too long!

Condo Characters

At any given moment in Florida, thousands of people are thinking about buying a condominium.

Couples from the Midwest who have just married off their last child, buried the family pet, and cashed in their last CD, are thumbing through local real estate guidebooks searching for their little slice of paradise. Floridians who have grown weary of battling weeds, keeping the pool in perfect balance, and avoiding the wacky neighbors next door, are shopping for a condo because their house is just "too much work anymore."

Whatever the motivating factor, they will scout out dozens of developments, explore an endless string of apartments with white walls and neutral carpeting, and look longingly at 3-by-6-foot balconies, saying "wouldn't that be the perfect place for our morning cups of coffee!"

They will grab their reading glasses and pour over scads of blueprints, trying to figure out whether their king-size bedroom furniture would fit in a 9-by-11 foot bedroom, and what on earth they're going to do with the contents of their garage.

They will pick apart the monthly maintenance fee, wondering if they shouldn't just keep their present house and hire a gardener instead.

In the end they will throw caution to the wind, plunk down their entire life savings, and sign a 30-year mortgage, which they expect will outlast them by a good dozen years.

And then they will meet ... **THE CONDO ASSO-CIATION FROM HELL!**

Their first lesson in condo living begins with a visit

from the condo association president, who is usually a retired military officer obsessed with running a "tight ship." This person, who was passed over for promotion and forced into early retirement, was elected on a platform of leadership.

Of course he ran unopposed because nobody else wanted the job. But now he's president for life. That's because it **IS** his life!

He issues orders, makes up petty rules, and polices the parking lot for cigarette butts. He lets you know if your car is parked outside the yellow lines, if it's dripping oil on the parking lot, or if it needs to be waxed. He'll even tell you what kind of wax you should use on your car, and berate you as a fool if you buy some inferior brand.

You can escape him by hiding out at the pool. But you better get there early if you want a chair. Each day many condo residents wake up at 6 a.m., hurry down to the pool, and place large towels on the lounge chairs to reserve them for later use. One of the first unwritten laws you need to learn at any condo is that towels indicate possession.

During the first month the new resident will probably attend a condo association meeting. Friends who live in condos tell me it's a good idea to attend these meetings on a regular basis, "just to protect what few rights you've got left."

At this meeting you will get acquainted with the lady in 3-F who is keeping a dog in her apartment, even though it is a clear violation of the condo association rules. She will make a case that her dog is 15 years old and has only a few good months left. Her appeal will be tabled, as it has been for the past four years.

You'll meet the man in 4-D who spends six hours a day

polishing his 15-year-old Cadillac and starts telling you about the classic car every time you get within six feet of him.

You'll be introduced to the widow in 2-B who grabs your arm, squeezes your hand, and invites you up to her apartment for a little drink after the meeting.

And you'll meet the condo manager, who takes you aside and tells you why he needs a raise.

But don't despair. You can always find refuge on your 3-by-6-foot balcony. As long as it's not overlooking all those towel-covered lounge chairs at the pool.

In The Dark
About Decorating

On the night I was born, interior decorators all over the world looked up in the sky, saw a cluster of stars in the shape of a dollar sign, and followed their instincts to my cradle.

When they arrived, the decorators gathered around me, lifted a glass of Dom Perignon to the heavens, and rejoiced.

"At last," they exclaimed to each other, "here is our ultimate customer. She won't be able to buy a pillow without a helping hand from us. She will make us rich beyond our wildest dreams."

"We have finally found a person with absolutely no ability to make a choice between sofas. A person who looks at a rack of fabric samples and breaks out in hives. A person who thinks primary colors are crayons used by first graders."

The decorators downed their champagne, piled order blanks and business cards at the foot of my crib, and departed with the knowledge that life would be good once I was old enough to own my own Visa card.

And it was so.

Since the time I left my crib, I have been at the mercy of interior decorators.

Granted, there were the early years of marriage when I tried to be creative with wood crates and throw pillows. But even then, the pillows I brought home from the thrift shop never seemed to go well with each other. And the crates always looked slightly out of place.

I discovered the joy of turning my problems over to an interior decorator when I was looking for my first sofa. There I was, trying to match orange fabric with green carpet, when a salesperson glanced over, rolled his eyes, and said, "Oh, no! Never!"

It was humiliating. I broke out in tears and fled from the store.

A friend led me to her decorator, and I dumped everything in her lap. That's where it has been ever since. If I have to match new carpet to an existing wallpaper, the decorator does the job. If I have to buy a new bedspread, the decorator makes the choice.

I'm not sure if it's a severe case of insecurity, or if my "good taste" genes were made inactive by some horrible DNA accident during my early development.

Whatever the reason, I long ago admitted to myself that without the help of an interior decorator, I would be living in a home resembling a Salvador Dali painting.

Usually, my decorating has been a relatively easy task of patching up existing problems and matching new items to old color schemes. But when we moved into a new house, I had to tackle a complete makeover, and life became miserable.

Even with the help of my decorator, I couldn't seem to make the most basic decisions. Here was a chance to establish a whole new color scheme, and I couldn't choose the colors.

"When you were a child and you had a new box of crayons, which color did you reach for first?" my decorator asked patiently, trying to lead me to a decision after weeks of vacillation.

I thought this was a great game until she wouldn't accept black for an answer.

The next day she dumped a pile of home decorating magazines on my table and said, "Look through these and call me when you see something you like."

What an eye-opener. I've never seen anything like it.

There are people in this world who have taste that's even more bizarre than my own. People who live in rooms that are entirely one color ... carpet, drapes, furniture, even the nightgown carefully thrown on the bed. People who hang paintings a foot above the baseboard. People who mix floral prints like I mix cake batter. And people who evidently redecorate their homes ... from basement to attic ... every three years, whether they need it or not.

The magazines are full of glossy photos showing people reclining on chaise longues, eating bon bons, while fluffy little dogs sit at their feet. They are designed for readers who actually enjoy choosing sofas and thumbing through wallpaper books and comparing fabric swatches.

The more I looked, the more I realized that the world of decorating is in a different galaxy from my world. I picked out a few colors, turned the whole thing over to my decorator, and said, "Call me when it's time to come home."

They say beauty is in the eyes of the beholder. I maintain it's in the eyes of interior decorators, and I've got a houseful of furniture to prove it.

The Root Of
The Dental Problem

I'm seriously considering quitting my job and hiring myself out as a national dental consultant.

Never has there been a void ... or cavity ... that screamed out so desperately to be filled. We're talking someone with just a little common sense advice to make each victim ... I mean patient ... breathe a little easier. Why I see a potential silver mine here.

The very first thing to go from virtually every dentist's office I'd consult with is the awful unmistakable smell.

Give me musk, give me Giorgio or give me potpourri, but please douse the place with something to cover up that awful dental odor. This may be a golden opportunity for some entrepreneur to market "dental deodorant." It only makes scents.

Next on my list of suggestions is to knock out that little

sliding glass window separating the receptionist from the rest of the world. You walk in the door, go to the window, and wait for the receptionist to look up, slide the little window open, and ask what you want.

I once asked a dental receptionist why she hid behind the little glass window. "Are you afraid some crazed gunman is going to burst in here and demand all your dental floss?" I asked. "Just what are you hiding from?"

She just looked up at me, rolled her eyes, and said, "Have you signed the check-in sheet?"

Suggestion number three: inject a little humor, or at least resort to laughing gas.

Then there are those stupid magazines stacked up in sloppy piles on the waiting room table. Issues like the spine-tingling "National Dental Health Weekly" or the sensual "Hygiene Hotline." Occasionally, if you're lucky, you'll find a four-year-old issue of "Reader's Digest."

I'd chuck those boring publications and subscribe to something spicy to get your mind off that torture chamber you're about to enter. Something to transport you to a balmy secluded beach ... on a starry night ... with that special someone. You get the picture. Something you can really sink your teeth into.

Next comes a desperately needed ironclad rule: No patient should be seated in the electric ... I mean dental ... chair until the dentist is ready to walk into the room. No more sitting there for half an hour in a pool of sweat listening to the humming drill in the next room, praying that each irregular pounding beat of your heart does not prove to be your last.

The only exception would be for all those brilliant patients smart enough to demand that heavenly nitrous oxide. "Happy gas" should be started at least half an hour in advance so that by the time the dentist arrives, you couldn't care less.

As you float on cloud nine, you can ponder the shapes of the water stains on the ceiling tiles (an integral part of every dental office) or count the number of flies, gnats and mosquitoes who have chosen the dentist's fluorescent lights as their final resting place. Which brings me to dental rule No. 2: A fastidious dynamite cleaning crew.

Now I don't know about you, but I'm pretty tired of dentists approaching me like I'm radiating leprosy. Honestly, I haven't spread malaria in months.

They walk in wearing their little masks and rubber gloves like they're about to crack a safe or rob you blind. And you leave without ever seeing their faces.

And it's about that tacky little napkin they adhere to your chest and promptly use as a garbage can. Yuck! Gross me out.

Now I'm not saying that all dentists need my help. In fact my new dentist is driving me crazy. She just doesn't fit the mold. She's young, vivacious and funny. She doesn't even hum!

She gives me gas. She doesn't hurt. She doesn't wear a mask. Her waiting room looks like a living room. And when you walk in, you choose which musical tape you want to listen to through your earphones while you're in "the chair."

Personally, I find it downright disconcerting. It's against my religion to befriend a dentist. It somehow goes against my nature.

But I find myself liking this girl, and even making plans to get together for lunch. Good Lord! I just hope she doesn't bring her own tartar sauce!

Hell On Wheels

Please, Lord, it can't be true!

For years I've dreaded this moment. It's given me terror-filled nightmares. My overwhelming fear of childbirth pales in comparison.

I've aged 35 years in the past three days. I already knew in my heart that it had to happen. But so soon!

That horrible dream has become a reality. My older daughter just got her learner's permit. She's driving a car!

"Ha," you say. "No big deal."

Don't say I didn't warn you. If she's anything like her mother, you'd better grab all those who are near and dear, evacuate immediately, and flee to the safety of the North for the next year.

I know whereof I speak. That phrase "hell on wheels" was coined the day I learned to drive. Well, actually the night before.

It all began one fateful night in June more than three decades ago when my parents were out for the evening. I was scheduled for my first lesson with a driving instructor the next day and, quite honestly, I was embarrassed to meet him with absolutely no experience under my belt.

All my friends had either practiced with their parents or snuck out in their family car. I was starting cold turkey. How humiliating!

But on that warm June night it suddenly occurred to me that there was a golden opportunity just sitting in the garage. My parents were out. Nobody was around. What harm could come if I just backed the car out of the garage

31

and turned it around in the driveway ... just to get the feel of it?

I grabbed the keys, walked up the hill to the garage behind our house, and settled into the seat of my mother's brand new Cadillac.

Cautiously I started the ignition, put it in reverse, and ever so slowly inched out of the garage. I backed the car around, carefully missing the basketball post, and headed it down the long, sloping driveway.

What a snap! Whatever was I worried about? I'd be terrific the next day.

I backed the car up the driveway, turned it around, and slipped it back into the garage. Perfect. Couldn't be better. Well, perhaps I could do it a little faster.

I thought I would try one more time, just to get it down pat.

Confidently I turned the key, put the car in reverse, and backed it around, turning the steering wheel long before I had cleared the garage. Big mistake.

The front door on the passenger side of the car had to be replaced, but luckily they were able to pound out the dents and repaint the back door and rear fender. And when they put in the new frame for the garage door and re-stuccoed the right side of the garage wall, you couldn't tell anything had ever happened.

For some reason my parents didn't look upon the entire situation in such a positive light. Even though I spent weeks with the driving instructor and passed my test on the first try, they were somehow reluctant to let me drive solo. I couldn't understand it. I was crushed. It was mortifying. It made no sense. What I needed was experience.

Finally my mother gave in. She would allow me to

drive to my friend's house, pick her up, and then head to a summer concert, but only if she (ma mere) were sitting beside me in the front seat. Ugh!

Beggars can't be choosers, so off we went with my stomach in knots and my mother breathing down my neck while embedding her white knuckles deeply into the padded dashboard.

I drove up my friend's long driveway, picked her up, and decided to take a shortcut through the back alley. There was a sharp right-hand blind turn into the narrow alley, and I knew I hadn't swung the car around the turn quite wide enough when my mother screamed, "Debby! Watch out! You're going to scrape that hedge."

I swung a little wider, but it was too late. Hidden in the 10-foot hedge was a telephone pole with one of those steel rungs peeking through the bushes, just waiting to grab hold of my mother's new car door.

After two accidents in two months, my mother was no longer willing to share her new Cadillac. So by default, I became the dubious owner of my grandmother's 11-year-old car. It looked like an Army tank, and was built like one, too.

Now that I think of it, the decision to give me that old car (fondly named "The Green Bomb") is probably the reason I am alive today. That and the fact that my father's many years as an insurance agent gave him the depth of understanding he needed to restrain himself from killing me with his two bare hands.

I had been driving for only four months when I had my third accident. I was returning home one afternoon about an hour later than promised. Naturally, I was in a hurry as I drove The Green Bomb up the driveway, which was about the length of a football field.

The garage was full, so I parked the car at the top of the driveway's incline where the hill flattened off. Well, almost flattened off.

I stopped the car, pulled the key out of the ignition, and started walking down the hill toward my house. The problem arose when the car did too.

Although the car was taking a leisurely roll backwards, the door that I hadn't shut tightly opened and gently knocked me to the ground. Then the car continued on its adventure off the driveway, over the lawn, through the hedge, into the neighbor's yard, down the hill, and through his flower garden, finally coming to rest against his ornamental light post, which was now leaning precariously over his stone wall, some six feet above his driveway.

I was stunned, and not because of my scratched knee. I was afraid to breathe for fear the light post would give way and the car would topple onto its head on the cement driveway.

The whole scenario presented a real challenge for the wrecking crew that had to retrieve my car. First they tried backing the tow truck through the neighbor's once-beautiful flower bed, but that did nothing but tear up the garden even more.

So what did they have to do? You guessed it ... follow the same meandering path The Green Bomb took, off the driveway, over the lawn, through the hedge, down the hill, and into the remaining flowers. And the two vehicles had to take the same path out, too.

I never forgot to put the car in park again. I also never spoke to the neighbors.

It was months before my next fiasco. I was driving down a narrow street. As I turned my head to talk to my friend in the passenger's seat, The Green Bomb seized the opportunity to take off on its own, right into a car parked on the opposite side of the street. I was so afraid to tell my parents that I momentarily considered leaving the scene. But that was academic. My car's fender was locked together with the parked car, and nobody was going anywhere.

To this day I swear my final mishap wasn't really my fault. I was driving on the interstate when a blinding rainstorm hit. Not wanting to take any chances, I decided to get off at the next exit.

Visibility was nil, but I did see the car in front of me suddenly hit the brakes. I was pretty far behind the car, but when I jammed my brake pedal, that old Green Bomb started to hydroplane and came to rest gently but firmly in the rear of the big black car.

I still didn't realize the gravity of the situation until the driver of the car started walking towards me in a dripping wet chauffeur's uniform. I instantly calculated the dollars it would take to repair the limousine and started praying for lightning to strike me on the spot.

I never found out who was in the back seat behind those darkened windows. I only know the mystery person was very understanding and said it was nobody's fault.

That evening must have changed my luck. It has been up hill from there. Five accidents in the first year, and only two minor problems in the next 30 years, neither of which were my fault. And you wonder why I laugh every time the driver's license bureau designates me a "safe driver."

But now the cycle is about to begin again. My daughter meets the driving instructor next week. Heaven help us!

A Broad Abroad

Climb every mountain? Give me a break!

Alpine Europe wasn't made for Floridians. When you haven't climbed a single step in the last decade and the only hills you ever encounter are constructed by fire ants, it should come as no shock when your leg muscles scream out in terror at the sight of a majestic Alp.

Is it any wonder why they have so many breathtakingly beautiful churches in Europe? It's so frantic tourists can get down on their hands and knees and beg for the strength to make it up — and down — the next hill.

When our family traded in our sea legs for the more sturdy mountain variety during a European vacation, we found ourselves dropping like flies over every curb, step, and cobblestone.

The adventure started off in a huge, screaming-orange VW bus that we rented at the Frankfort airport. The bus had a standard transmission, which would have been fine had it worked and if the roads there had been a little wider than your typical tourist class airline seat.

But nooooo. Within six hours the vehicle had totally broken down and we had succeeded in denting the entire left side while attempting to park it in an indoor garage the size of a thimble.

The adventure went from bad to worse the next day. We got a new, smaller car and were off to the Alps, where we hopped a chair lift for a scenic trip high — and I mean **HIGH** — up into the mountains. We hiked to a remote but beautiful glacial lake, where we spotted a gorgeous waterfall.

Drawn like a magnet, my husband — with daughter in

one hand and my new camera in the other — started up the rocky stream bed to the base of the waterfall. Well, they don't call them falls for nothing! My husband slipped and fell face-first into the icy stream.

My daughter escaped injury, but my husband's two front teeth, his mouth, shoulder and foot weren't so lucky. Neither was my camera.

His smile was as jagged as the cliffs. His skin was as blue as the lake. But that night he took my nail file to his teeth and his smile was as good as new.

There's no experience quite like dining out in Europe. It starts with making reservations in a language you don't understand, and it ends when you get down on your knees and beg for the check. In between, it's pure experiment.

When you call a restaurant and try to reserve a table in a language you don't speak, you're never quite sure what the person on the other end of the phone is telling you. He could be reserving a table for two at 8:30. He could be telling you the health inspector just ran off with the chef. He could be telling you his restaurant doesn't serve swine. But he won't be telling you, "We can't wait to have you dine with us."

And you're never really certain that you've actually arrived at the restaurant, even though you've got a slip of hotel stationery with the address held tightly in your fist. The taxi driver has dropped you off in the middle of a street, collected the equivalent of 400 American dollars, and pointed you in the direction of old buildings that could be warehouses, whorehouses, or people's houses. None of the structures has a sign out front flashing RESTAURANT in neon letters.

If you're lucky enough to find an address number

posted on the outside of one of the buildings, you go inside, sit down, and are handed a menu you can't read. You might as well be interpreting the secret design plans for a Soviet nuclear submarine ... in Russian.

For an American whose only foreign language is Pig Latin, coming face-to-face with a foreign menu can bring on a complete anxiety attack.

The average European menu looks something like this:

La pottage du fromage en porage — 186pq 14s
Bloodwurst mit hockpuie — 5731 39sf
Wiener schnitzel ad nausea — 427mn 9st
Phxuzrptilmburtzyhtck — 27 b.c.
Kaffee - 839L
Coca Cola — $9,326,748 (American dollars only)

When the waiter finally strolls over to your table, he frowns. European waiters have this uncanny ability to spot American tourists even before we utter a word. I suspect it's either our tennis shoes or our cameras.

Naturally, you want to appear suave and sophisticated. So you don't ask the already haughty waiter to translate every item on the menu. Instead, you point to one selection and say, "This sounds good" with as much enthusiasm as you can muster.

As soon as the waiter leaves, you panic. What if you ordered ox entrails steamed in camel sweat!

You'll have plenty of time to worry about your selection. The waiter won't be back for at least an hour, leaving you with only an empty glass that once contained warm water, and a hard piece of bread with no butter. (That must be how Europeans cut down on cholesterol.)

Since none of the above menu items sound too entic-

ing, and the special of the day was roughly translated by the waiter as "pork nostrils with gypsy sauce," I frequently opted for the familiar sounding wiener schnitzel.

Dining in Europe is a leisurely experience. That's sometimes difficult for impatient Americans to comprehend. You can stare at your empty plate (if you were actually able to devour the ox entrails) for hours before the waiter clears the table.

Then comes the coffee (if you can afford it) and the dessert. In a land that produces heavenly hot chocolate and candy bars you could die for, chocolate desserts are at a premium. My favorite chocolate concoction was (I swear I'm not making this up) Mozart's balls.

If you don't beg for the check immediately following dessert, you could be in for another hour of leisurely sitting. Then it's back to the hotel. If you're lucky, you'll get the same taxi driver who brought you to the restaurant five hours earlier. He knows where you're staying. That's good, because you don't.

Before I went to Europe, I would have defined "customs" as uniformed men who get their kicks going through other people's luggage. Now I know that customs really means the way the other half lives.

I'm sure the advertising executive who came up with the phrase, "Aren't you glad you use Dial? Don't you wish everyone did?" had just returned from a summer trip abroad.

I knew European women didn't shave, but this particular problem came as quite a shock to me. After a lot of thought, I've come up with a number of theories as to why this stinking problem exists:

Reason No. 1: Europeans don't use washcloths. I stayed in fancy hotels with every amenity known to man, but there was not a washcloth in sight. At first I assumed it was a mistake as I dunked a bath towel in the tub. But no way! It happened night after night, even in hotels bearing American names like Ramada.

Reason No. 2: There are 5,387,648 different types of sinks, showers, and toilets in Europe, each of which takes a person with an advanced degree in physics to figure out how to operate.

I kid you not. There are **tiny** little tubs with seats built in which, when properly filled with water, will soak the area of your body from the soles of your feet to mid-calf.

There are showers with thermostats and two shower heads which, after a half-hour of experimenting and three calls to the front desk, I never did figure out.

And there are thousands of bathrooms in Europe with

40

showers but no shower curtains. That's real convenient if you want to go for a quick swim after you bathe and are too lazy to walk to the swimming pool. These particular showers are often equipped with disposable shower caps designed, I suspect, to cover the roll of toilet paper located across the bathroom.

Then of course there are the bidets, which I must confess I never did master because no two ever worked the same way.

Now for the potties. Frankly, I thought I had seen it all in Florida the night I discovered those magic toilet seats encased in plastic that actually rotate in a circle around the potty until they are completely covered with a new sheet of plastic. Will wonders never cease?

Apparently not! Europe had its own collection of sitters and squatters. However the most memorable was a stainless steel floor with a hole in the middle. This little wonder — for women, mind you — had no manual flushing device, but was instead activated by an electric eye as soon as it was put to use. Get real! For the money they spent on that little number, I would have preferred a standard working toilet.

But the real marvels of Europe are the sinks. There are regular sinks, sinks that are activated by pushing a dot on the floor, and sinks that magically dispense water the minute you put your hands under the faucet.

But my all time favorite sink is located in a restaurant in Bern, Switzerland. You may think I'm exaggerating, but I swear I'm not making this up. You walk up to this small porcelain box on the wall and stick your hands inside the box. First the tiny genie inside turns on warm water. Then it stops. Next, just the right amount of soap is automatically dispensed. After you have time to rub your hands together and work up a lather, the water automatically starts again for the final rinse. And then, the piece de resistance, out blows the hot air to dry your hands. All in one little machine!

Reason No. 3: Bathrooms are simply not a high priority item in Europe. The exquisite French palace of Versailles, for example, was built without a single bathroom. Does that tell you anything? No wonder the perfume industry got such an early start!

Furthermore, I'm fairly convinced there is a rule written in stone that the few public rest rooms they do have must be located **A.**) in the dungeon, or **B.**) down a minimum of five flights of stairs.

These "facilities" are invariably "attended" by crazed men and women with the look of the Wicked Witch of the West and the personality of Attila the Hun. These people are required to be honor graduates of the Mafia School of Hit Men. "You Don't Pay ... You Better Pray" is the motto engraved in their revolvers. The idea is that if you value your life, you should toss into the dish a random unidentifiable amount of generic European money and not look back, even when you return to your hotel and discover you gave the bathroom attendant the equivalent of 134 American dollars.

Now for the fourth, but no less important, explanation for the bad odor problem: They don't do A.C. over there.

The hotels don't have air conditioning. Neither do the restaurants or the cars. What on earth must they be thinking? Sure, they have snow falling on the mountain tops in July. But in the valleys on the lake in the shade, it's still 98 degrees.

To make matters worse, there's another bizarre little custom that would be heavenly in the winter but which

I found pure Hell in the summer heat. Europeans don't do sheets!

Let me explain. On every bed the bottom sheet is tucked under the mattress like in America. But instead of a top sheet, blanket and bedspread, the Europeans substitute a beautiful thick down comforter enclosed in a giant pillowcase. On a cool night — say 25 degrees — this little number is heaven on earth. But on a hot, humid summer night, you don't wake up smelling like you've slept in a bed of roses ... if you get my drift!

Financial Misnomers

When the word "Depression" is mentioned, why does it usually have the word "Great" in front of it?

What was so great about the Depression? I wasn't around to actually experience it, but from all that I've read, it didn't sound so great to me.

It wasn't even "good." If I were in charge, I would have called it the "Horrendous Depression" or the "Grim Depression." But never "Great."

Of course I've always had a problem with financial terminology. People who deal with financial affairs (and I don't mean of the heart) speak a different language.

Be honest. Do you really know what a no-load mutual fund is? Or zero-base coupons? It's beyond me.

One time I was flipping through a news magazine and came across a headline that said, "A Good Time for Convertibles." Naturally, I stopped to read the story, figuring it would be about riding through the country-side with the top down, the wind blowing through your hair.

What a shock to find that "convertible" is another term for a bond that can be exchanged for common stock.

"The convertible protects you against the volatility of the market," the article stated. And all this time I thought a convertible protected you against becoming old and stodgy.

What do the simple folk do when it comes to investing? They throw up their hands in frustration and run toward their piggy bank, which doesn't speak any language and is therefore easier to understand.

As a public service to everyone who actually thinks cold, hard cash means money that has just been removed from the freezer, I'm about to offer useful financial terminology that you can use to dazzle your friends and relatives.

Here are just a few definitions you can study. Learn them and some day you, too, may be able to figure out the difference between broke and broker.

Accrual System: What a Southern man calls the group of financial institutions that refused to loan him the money for his new car, as in "That's a cruel system of money lenders."

Prime Rate: This isn't actually a financial term. It is really the price the supermarket charges for prime beef. But the beef is usually served to bankers and brokers at lunch, so it has slipped into their vocabulary and even reported by "The Wall Street Journal," an extremely boring newspaper that contains no comic section.

Demand Deposit: Financial institutions, according to the Federal Omnibus Banking and Stick-It-To-'Em Law of 1937, have the power to demand that any person residing within a five-mile radius of the facility has to keep deposits at that facility. Thus the term "demand deposit."

Balance Of Payments: This is what the typical owner of a credit card does when the monthly bill arrives and it says "You Owe The Bank $2,846,947," and the person has only $2.94 in his checking account."

Bank Draft: Sometimes those electric doors on banks get stuck in the open position. That's when you use the term "bank draft."

Reg E: Great music from the Caribbean that is almost never played in the lobbies of financial institutions.

Cancelled Checks: This is what I wish I could do when I accidentally write a check for more than I have in my account. But instead of cancelling the check, the bank pays it and then sends me an overdraft bill in the amount of what I would probably pay for a semester's tuition at Yale.

Checkless Society: A banker's nightmare. If there were no checks, there would be no overdrafts. That means no overdraft fees. That means the banker would have to eat chicken instead of steak for lunch. Talk about the Great Depression!

Compound: Sometimes, when the bank won't loan you money, you can borrow from loan sharks. Compound is a term they use when referring to repayment schedules, as in "you'll have a compound fracture if the money isn't in my hands by Tuesday." Also, refer to "face value."

Fiduciary: I don't know what this word actually means, but I've always liked the sound of it.

Credit Crunch: The brand name of cereal bankers eat

for breakfast.

Frozen Asset: This term is used only in Alaskan financial circles, so forget you've ever heard it.

General Ledger: The head of the World Bank is General Francisco Ledger. General Ledger is from one of those Third World nations, which is why all the American banks loaned money to countries you never heard of, and now they can't afford to loan you any money. Blame it on General Ledger.

Garnishment: A nice little touch of green placed on a plate at lunch. Sometimes they use "escrow" for the garnishment.

Over And Short Account: When a child walks into a bank to open his first savings account, the teller looks **over** the counter and sees a **short** customer wanting to open an **account**.

That's about it. If you believe any of these definitions, I've got a nice convertible in the parking lot I'd like to sell you.

Parable Of The Fishes

In the beginning, there was an empty fish tank. And it was free.

"Take this tank and use it, in remembrance of me," my father said as he was cleaning out his garage one day.

On the first day we filled it with water ... 30 gallons of water ... water teeming with tiny little particles that make you wonder "just what is this stuff I'm pouring into my stomach?"

On the second day we purchased a filter at a cost of $39.95, for the water was green and the tank slimy.

On the third day we analyzed the water with a deluxe test kit ($8.99) and found too much ammonia and not enough pH. But $12 worth of chemicals solved that problem.

On the fourth day we created an underwater world, with plastic plants and bright blue gravel, and it was beautiful. It was also $21.75.

On the fifth day we purchased a top ($21) for the aquarium to prevent future inhabitants from jumping out and perishing on the carpet.

On the sixth day we added a thermometer, a heater, and a neon light (total $34.95) because The Book ($7.95) said it was so.

And on the seventh day there were fish ... three swordtails (named Larry, Daryl and Daryl) and two neons (too small to have names).

On the eighth day we rested, counting our investment.

On the ninth day we were watching the fish eat their dinner when some of the food suddenly swam away.

"They had babies!" my daughter screamed.

And The Book says, "They shall eat their babies if you don't put them in a separate tank." And it was so.

By 3 a.m. of the tenth day, we had rescued seven microscopic fish and they were living in the tank in my kitchen sieve, separated from their hungry parents by a thin sheet of Saran wrap.

The rest were eaten alive!

"The Book says these fish usually have 75 to 100 babies as a time," my daughter said. At 3 a.m., seven out of 100 doesn't seem like bad odds!

In the words of the pet store manager, "You need a breeding tank." And it costs $10.95.

But when we put the baby fish in the breeding tank, three of them swam out through the slots in the bottom and were promptly gobbled up by the bigger fish.

"Then I guess you need this smaller breeding tank," the pet store manager said. And it was so.

On the eleventh day we added two guppies and a mollie, and on the twelfth day one of the guppies died. Luckily, guppies come with a seven-day guarantee, and so it was replaced.

On day 13, two fish took on a fuzzy white appearance, and it caused grave concern throughout the land. On day 14 those fish were found floating, belly up, near the top of the tank. And there was great remorse.

"What can be wrong?" we asked the pet store prophet, handing him a baggy containing two furry dead fish.

"Too much ammonia," he said in a voice that reverberated throughout the store. And customers shook their heads and fish in 48 different tanks became visibly nervous.

"And you've got the wrong kind of filter," he added. "Your tank is too big for that little filter."

He refused to sell us any more fish until we solved our problem, and behind him I could hear thousands of little guppies gurgle with relief.

Midway through the third week, our water was proclaimed "passable" and we joined the Fish Club and collected our free fish of the month from the local pet store.

And the free fish had to have a mate. And the mate had a price tag of $5.95. And we had a tank of many colors.

In one month we went from five fish to more than 100

(although only 14 survived), and from a free tank to equipment worth more than $175.

Talk about the loaves and the fishes!

Par For The Course

I've got a word of warning for all you golfers: **WATCH YOUR LANGUAGE!**

My house is located on the sand trap right next to the dog-leg on the sixth fairway, and I can't believe the words I hear coming from your mouths!

What is it about golf that drives you into such a frenzy?

Is it the loss of the $375 you paid for all the golf balls you left in my yard?

Or the embarrassment of having to wear funny looking pants and a hat that belongs on Bugs Bunny?

Maybe it's the stress of riding around in those little electric carts that take off with a jerk, causing extreme anxiety and occasional whiplash, while you really want to be back at the club house sloshing down drinks.

Whatever the cause, I've never witnessed such frustration as I've seen on the golf course.

As I understand it, the sole purpose of golf is to swing a club somewhere in the vicinity of a little ball, hoping it will go into a little hole.

Toward that objective, some crazy Scot invented some odd-shaped sticks (known either by numbers, such as the nine iron, or by names so ridiculous even an avid golfer has a hard time actually saying them ... brassie, mashie, whoopie, etc.) with which to hit the ball.

The sticks are packaged in an elaborate golf bag that is too heavy for the average human to carry around on his shoulder, unless he's been taking steroids. And in that case he's a serious athlete, pumping iron at the gym all weekend instead of playing at some sissy sport like golf.

From my window I've observed that golfers usually take two or three practice swings before actually hitting the ball. Those swings always take the shape of a perfect arc.

When golfers get serious about hitting the ball, the swing takes on an entirely different shape. Usually the club digs into the ground, sending grass and dirt flying high in the air. Often the golf ball will fly, too ... for about 25 feet or so.

Then the golfer will say a few really bad words, throw his hat on the ground, shake his fist wildly, slam his club into the bag, and jump into the golf cart for a 15-second ride to the ball's new location.

Occasionally the ball will take flight, only to hit a tree 40 feet away. Such an occurrence will really cause consternation for the golfer, who will jump up and down screaming.

With a little luck, golfers usually make it to the green. For you non-golfers, that's the area of short green grass where the little hole is located. It's usually surrounded by sand piles, man-made lakes, or other unnatural hazards.

To get a better understanding of the game, I once attended a professional golf tournament that featured middle-aged overweight men who did not appear to be having a really fun time, despite the fact that they were playing to win an amount of money greater than the

entire Third World debt.

For a non-golfer, viewing a professional golf tournament is about as exciting as watching a tank full of tropical fish.

Several thousand spectators (also dressed, I might add, in funny looking pants and hats) lined the fairway in silence. If someone spoke above a whisper, a tournament official would give the spectator a very stern glare.

The silence was broken by occasional bursts of applause arising from the crowd after a golfer sank a putt. The spectators apparently acted without the aid of an applause sign. It was exciting!

One of these days I just may take up golf ... after the tropical fish die.

It's A Wonderful Life

Her Story:

Why am I the only one in this house who knows how to operate the washing machine?

It's not like it takes an engineering degree. All you do is turn a few dials. A 10-year-old could do it.

And how come nobody else knows how to fold clean clothes after they come out of the dryer? I could dump them in the middle of the living room floor and the rest of the family would walk around the pile for weeks before anyone would notice.

Why does everyone in the family think I know where things are kept? "Mom, where's my brush?" "Honey, have you seen my keys?" "Mommy, where are my shoes?" The odd thing is, I usually know just where to find the things they're looking for.

When I walk through the house, I see wet glasses leaving rings on wood tables, stray shoes and socks, grape jelly smudges on the sliding glass doors, newspapers scattered all over the furniture, and leftover grass from the Easter basket buried in the carpet. Why doesn't anyone else see these things ... and take care of them?

If I weren't around, the dog would probably starve to death. Perhaps that's why she is so loving to me but ignores the rest of the family.

And what about the rest of the family? They'd starve to death, too. Not one of them knows how to get a pork chop out of the refrigerator. When they open that door, all they see is soft drinks and snack food. I doubt they would recognize any form of uncooked food that contained an ounce of nutrition. Ask them what they would like for dinner and all I get is a blank stare.

Speaking of the refrigerator, if the kids happen to knock over an open can of cola while they are searching for the cheese, they never seem to notice the liquid pouring out and spilling from shelf to shelf like a mountain waterfall. They just grab the cheese and close the door.

My husband is no help. If he isn't reading, I know I can find him working in the yard. You'd think he'd want to spend some time with his family. And the children only have eyes for the television set.

I think I'm going crazy!

His Story:

Why am I the only one in this house who knows how to operate the lawn mower?

It's not like it takes an engineering degree to cut the grass. All it takes is a little sweat. A 10-year-old could do it.

And how come nobody else knows how to pull weeds or trim bushes in the garden? The weeds could be growing so high you couldn't get through the front door and the rest of the family would walk around to the back door to get in the house.

Why are things never in their proper place? The kids can never find their shoes. And my keys are never where they're supposed to be. Everything is so disorganized. Why can't everybody just learn to put things where they belong?

And why am I the only person who ever takes out the garbage. If I weren't around, the house would fill up with garbage and nobody would notice.

When I walk through the house, I see dust balls, dirty dishes, smeared windows, discarded newspapers, and empty potato chip bags. Isn't anybody trying to keep this house clean? Why there's even leftover grass from the Easter basket buried in the carpet.

And I'm sick of having to barbecue pork chops on the grill every night. Why can't we have something new and different for dinner. My wife's got hundreds of cookbooks. Why doesn't she read some of them?

The kids load up on cola and junk food all day long. If there were something good for dinner, maybe their eating habits wouldn't be so bad.

And another thing. There are never clean socks when I want them. Dirty clothes are overflowing from the laundry basket and I'm always running out of clean shirts. Somebody needs to keep up with those household chores, and it's not me. I've got too much yard work to do.

I think I'm going crazy!

The 10-Year-Old's Story:

Why am I the only one in this house who knows how to wash dirty dishes?

It's not like there's a commandment that says "children shall wash the dishes." Hasn't anybody ever heard of child labor laws?

If Daddy didn't spend so much time pulling weeds and Mommy didn't fuss over the dog so much, maybe they'd have more time for me. We could play Monopoly, and I would have something better to do than watch TV all day long.

And they think everything should be so clean all the time! If one toy ends up on the floor, you'd think the sky was falling. I don't understand why they're such fanatics.

How was I supposed to know wet glasses leave rings

on wood tables? And my sister just forgot she was holding a peanut butter and jelly sandwich in the same hand she used to open the door for the dog. What's the big deal?

When I walk through the house, all I hear is "Don't leave your toys there," and "Pick up your shoes," and "Did you make your bed?" and "Clean up that mess you made." Why do I have to do everything? They wouldn't even let me store my Easter eggs under the sofa. It's not as if the Easter grass is actually going to start growing in the carpet!

And if I have to eat another Brussel sprout, I think I'll puke. Why can't Mom fix something good for dinner? It's always weird things like cauliflower and wontons and liver. Whatever happened to hamburgers?

I think I'm going crazy!

The Dog's Story:

Why am I the only one in this house who knows how to relax? It's not like the world's going to end if the clothes don't get washed or the grass gets too long. What's the big deal?

If they didn't all spend so much time working, maybe they'd have time to play catch with me. All I do all day long is sit around and wait for some attention. Is that asking too much?

And I'm sick of that dog food! If they'd just buy me some nice hamburger, I'd be one happy dog.

Another thing. How come these people are always losing things? They can never find their shoes or their keys or their brushes. Maybe they've just got too much to take care of. I've never once lost my ball.

I think they're all crazy!

A Shortage Of
Mr. Goodwrench Hormones

I'm married to a man who has an abnormally low count of Mr. Goodwrench hormones.

When all the other boys in eighth grade shop class were building knickknack shelves and learning how to use a pipe wrench, he was trying to figure out how to open his pencil box.

While his teenage friends were dismantling car engines and figuring out how they worked, he was still trying to figure out the difference between the ignition key and the trunk key.

The Scouts actually held a formal ceremony and revoked his woodworking badge.

His lack of Mr. Goodwrench hormones has led to a lot of frustration during the years of our marriage ... mainly **MY** frustration. You see, he recognizes his limitations, but that never stops him from meddling with some task he should leave to the experts.

I remember the month when he tried (and failed) to repair three major items from your basic household appliance group. It was a particularly trying time.

When water started pouring out from the base of the kitchen faucet handle as well as the spigot, the plumber gland started to secrete some sort of chemical in my husband's brain that made him think he was capable of fixing the problem.

"It's probably just a washer," he said, which surprised me because this is a man who can't even figure out which clothes go in the dark load and which go in the

white load.

By the time he had replaced the faucet washer, he had also replaced the entire cartridge, to the tune of $15.95. But somehow things got a little mixed up.

When I turned the handle to cold, hot water flowed from the faucet. When I turned the handle to hot, cold water came out. And each time I turned on the water, it poured out of the base of the faucet at an increasingly alarming rate.

"Let's see if it gets better after a few days," he said, shutting off the faucet and leaving the kitchen. I find he frequently relies on this "leave it alone and see if it goes away" philosophy.

Within days the water started dripping down through the counter top, and soon the cabinet under the sink began to look like a swimming pool. Sponges started to float around, and cleanser cans began to rust.

Eventually the plumber had to install a new faucet, turning a 50-cent washer replacement into a $125 expense.

Several days later my husband was walking around the side of our house and saw water dripping from the eaves. And it wasn't even raining.

The dripping water started those old glands flowing, and before I knew what was happening, my husband was up in the attic inspecting the air conditioner unit.

Now I get real nervous any time he ventures up in the attic, but when he's got a tool box under his arm, I can see only disaster ahead.

"Please don't!" I implored as he lined up a screw driver and started to disassemble the unit. Luckily, common sense (or the hot attic atmosphere) got the better of him and he stopped before he did any serious damage. At least that's what the air conditioner repairman said when he came to my rescue later that afternoon.

Over the years I've learned a few things.

I never let my husband visit a hardware store unaccompanied. That policy alone has saved me thousands of dollars in repair bills.

I steer him away from the home-repair books whenever we're in a bookstore. He starts salivating at the sight of those "How To" titles, and it's best not to get him started.

At Christmas time I assemble all the kids' presents while my husband is at work. Otherwise, Santa wouldn't be able to stop at our house.

For his birthday last year I gave my husband a tool box. In it were the yellow page listings for the plumber, the electrician, and Mr. Goodwrench.

Those are the only tools he needs!

It's The Little Things That Drive You Crazy!

For all those couples who are considering marriage, let me give you a warning. No matter how happy you are with each other today, the little things are going to drive you crazy!

You may not believe me now because love is blind. But all those little personality quirks you overlook before the wedding will come back to haunt you.

When you're dating a man who is deliberate and precise, for example, you're in awe of his patience and perseverance.

When you're engaged to a man who is deliberate and precise, you think to yourself, "What wonderful traits your children will inherit."

During the first month of marriage to a man who is

deliberate and precise, you laugh to yourself about how long it takes him to install a paper towel holder.

After the first year of marriage to a man who is deliberate and precise, you begin to wonder if you can really spend the rest of your life with a man who is so obsessed with uncurling phone cords and lining up screws so the slots all head the same direction.

I speak from experience. My husband is efficient, orderly and systematic. On the day we were married, when the priest asked him about the ring, my husband pulled a little velvet box out of his pocket, took the ring out, carefully folded the sales receipt and stuck it back in his pocket before putting the ring on my finger.

I should have realized then that I was marrying a man who would devote his life to organizing my kitchen cabinets, filing my recipes, and generally making my life miserable.

When he wraps the last 15 feet of a roll of wax paper around a new roll so he can throw the empty box away and save four square inches in the kitchen cupboard, I can no longer see any humor in the situation.

When he gets in my car and spends five minutes readjusting the seat, the mirror, the seat belt and the radio, I have to stifle my urge to scream, "Put the key in the ignition and let's get going!"

You may be saying to yourself, "Sure, I recognize my lover's faults, but I'll be able to change those quickly enough. And besides, what I can't change I can live with."

Oh, the ignorance of youth!

Take it from me, no woman can learn to live with a man who never puts the seat of the toilet down after he's finished.

Trying to accommodate a person who pretends he doesn't hear a ringing telephone 10 feet away from his chair only makes you want to wrap the phone cord around his neck.

Try driving across the country with a man who will go the wrong direction for 250 miles rather than ask someone for directions and see if you can still laugh about it when you reach California.

I foolishly married a man who thinks his sole purpose in life is to organize the world. Everything he touches, he organizes.

Some of you are probably thinking, "She married the guy to compensate for her own lack of organization."

Not true! But at the time I did find it amusing that he had his books stacked in alphabetical order, and his record collection was indexed by category.

Never did I dream that one day his compulsiveness would drive me crazy.

Could you share your medicine closet with a person who lines up prescription bottles on the shelf in order of descending size?

Could you keep your temper while your spouse empties the contents of three half-eaten boxes of different crackers into a baggy and labels it "mix and match"?

I have actually seen this man combine half a jar of blue cheese salad dressing with half a jar of mayonnaise to save space in the refrigerator and then plead ignorance when the kids complain about the strange taste of their tuna salad sandwich.

He is not to be trusted!

The highlight of my husband's week is Wednesday night. That's because garbage pickup is Thursday morning.

While I sit in front of the television, my husband sweeps through the house searching for "garbage." Almost anything that isn't bolted down is fair game.

Hangars that are slightly bent are removed from the closet and tossed in the garbage.

Plastic wrapping is ripped from the clothes just back from the cleaners and goes out with the trash.

I've seen him take a magazine from my hands and say, "If you're through reading this, I'll put it in the garbage."

The refrigerator is searched with a keen eye. Jars that are only a quarter full are likely to disappear. If fruit has even a hint of brown, say "good-bye."

If the kids don't grab their homework assignments off the floor, they'll have to search through the garbage can the next morning on their way to school.

Anything that doesn't move is history. It's a miracle that our small dog (who spends a good deal of her life sleeping on the kitchen floor) hasn't been thrown into the trash by now.

One day I came home from the store and found my husband cleaning out the cabinet I keep spices in. He was in the middle of pouring the contents of one little container of nutmeg into a larger container of nutmeg when I exploded.

"Why are you doing this to me?" I shouted.

"Just trying to get you organized," he said, smiling.

"I don't want to be organized! I liked my spice cabinet the way it was. I don't want it in alphabetical order. Having two cans of nutmeg gives me a feeling of security. Leave it alone!"

"OK," he said sheepishly. "But I think you're being a little irrational about the whole thing."

After two decades of marriage, he still has all the qualities that drive me crazy!

Hot Flashes In Medicine

Terrorists and bombs make a deadly duo.

Saddam Hussein and poison gas threaten millions.

But there's no more lethal combination in this world than a few aches and pains, my vivid imagination, and a trusty ambiguous medical encyclopedia.

If you see us coming, don't bother heading for the hills. You might as well take the direct route right to the cemetery.

With my bargain basement medical book I can successfully diagnose your fatal disease long before you thought it was a remote possibility.

It's neither a matter of intuition nor a case of medical genius. Rather, it's an inherited trait passed down through the females of my family for generations.

My maternal grandmother was born with the knowledge that with her hot water bottle, her drum of castor oil, her boric acid eye bath, and her "miraculous" witch hazel, there was no disease known to man she couldn't diagnose and cure.

My paternal grandmother, on the other hand, thought that was ridiculous. Why everyone knew it was the enema that could dramatically cure any internal problems that Mercurochrome couldn't heal on the outside.

Vicks, calamine lotion, and baby powder are my mother's miracle drugs. And it is she — and her sister — who have genetically passed on "**the art of the diagnosis.**"

For my mother is the proud owner of not one, but two medical encyclopedias. The 20-volume number she purchased week-by-week at the A&P in, I believe, 1962. The other, a complete one-volume up-to-date family medical guide, was newly revised in 1980.

With these two infallible books of knowledge she can analyze, diagnose, and map out the most effective treatment for any family member, friend, casual acquaintance or neighbor's relative in the continental United States.

Years ago when my older daughter was sick, my pediatrician jokingly turned to my mother, who had just finished outlining her own diagnosis, and asked, "Just which medical school did you graduate from?"

But while my mother, aunt, and grandmothers can glean some ray of hope — no matter how trivial — from the worn and tattered pages of their medical books, I can find only doom and gloom.

No matter what the symptoms — headaches, stomach pains, sore throat, or bruises — there can be only one inevitable and unmistakable conclusion — CANCER!

My most recent brush with death came when my system went haywire. Since I would rather lie down in a colony of fire ants than go to a gynecologist, I did what any rational, educated coward would do. I ignored it in hopes it would go away.

But no!

Forced to resort to my medical encyclopedia, I imagined I had every symptom in the book.

Surely it couldn't be the early symptoms of **M-E-N-O-P-A-U-S-E!**

No, I'm much too young for that. Wasn't it only yesterday that I graduated from college, got married, and had kids?

Granted, lately my cycle has been as predictable as a hurricane. My memory is like a sieve. And if my mustache continues to grow at this rate, I'm going to wake up looking like Gene Shalit!

No. It couldn't be. My medical books were right. Panicked, positive my body was riddled with cancer, I went to the doctor.

Suffice it to say that in four months I was X-rayed more than the Shroud of Turin. They took enough blood to feed Florida's entire population of mosquitoes. And I slipped my heels into more stirrups than Princess Anne and her entire equestrian team.

All this to find out that it's nothing more than nature taking its course. What a fool I was!

The next time this happens, I'm not going to panic. I'm just going to slap on some Vicks, douse myself in witch hazel, have an enema and an eye bath, and forget it!

Moving Madness

My philosophy on cleaning house is simple: every three years I move.

It may sound a bit drastic, but it's effective. As soon as that "FOR SALE" sign goes up, my vacuum hits the floor in a feverish effort to remove three year's worth of dirt.

Moving every three years helps keep my life in order.

You see, for a hopelessly disorganized person like myself, things tend to accumulate.

Receipts and notes multiply into mountains of paper scattered throughout the house. Magazines and catalogs pile up into uncontrollable heaps. Items that should have been thrown away five minutes after they entered the house linger for years at a time.

Before you know it, the mess is out of control. Desperation sets in. You contemplate lighting a match and setting fire to the house as the only way out.

When you move every three years, you're forced to deal with the mess.

You have to make hard choices:

Will Aunt Matilda care if you give her wedding

present (a hideous purple vase) to the Goodwill?

Does a broken toaster-oven really have a life after death?

Are the jelly glasses in the closet really something I want to leave to my children when I die?

Questions like these should be dealt with on an every-day basis, but I'm the kind of person who puts off such decisions until another day.

The last time a "FOR SALE" sign went up in my front yard, I vacuumed the carpet hard enough to suck some of the color out of it. There was so much spray wax in the air my house smelled like a lemon grove.

Flecks of paint were scraped off the windows. Dead bugs were removed from the sliding glass door tracks. Leaves were flushed out of the gutters.

Then comes that moment when you look around and tell your spouse, "This house looks too good to sell. All the projects we've put off for the past three years are done. Why don't we just stay?"

But no, once a house is clean, it's time to move on and mess up another house. Never look back.

Next comes the hard part. We both get dressed up in solid, traditional homeowner clothes and, looking like Ozzie and Harriett, we greet prospective buyers with cookies and milk and patriotic songs.

We guide them around the impeccably clean house, pretending that we never leave newspapers lying around, always look through spotless windows, and constantly keep our refrigerator free of mold and leftovers.

The prospective buyers will be impressed with our clean woodwork, our orderly closets, and our organized cabinets. They'll be dazzled by our sparkling bathtub, and our weedless garden.

And they'll go home to their shabby abode, look around at the dust and grime, and wonder to themselves how they could live in such dirt and chaos. Then they'll put their house on the market, thus forcing themselves to undertake a massive cleanup campaign.

It's all part of the American dream ... or should I say nightmare?

At this very moment there are millions of Americans trying to sell a house. They say there's strength in numbers. I sense only despair.

The sign in the front yard can't begin to tell the story of what's going on inside. Behind all those freshly painted doors and neatly curtained windows, there's turmoil. Take my word for it!

The "FOR SALE" sign carries with it a change of life-style. You may be prepared to keep your house "clean" for months as people troop in and out, but "spotless" is another matter.

Suddenly, the junk under your bed becomes a problem. The dust on the lamp shades is a no-no. The far reaches of your oven (always before off limits) are fair game for inspection.

You have to smile politely as people you wouldn't want as neighbors stick their noses into closets where you just left a pile of dirty laundry.

You have to drive around town with your car's trunk full of stuffed animals just so your children's closets will look a little less cluttered.

You have to nod in agreement as ignorant intruders make plans to rip out your new $30-a-yard carpet and replace it with no-wax linoleum.

There is a way to avoid all this agony, thanks to good old American ingenuity. The solution is called a "lock box" and it's installed by your Realtor on your front door.

This little gimmick enables real estate agents to bring people into your house to view your dust balls even when you're not home.

There are, however, certain disadvantages. If there's a lock box on your front door, you spend most of your working hours worrying whether the kids remembered to flush the toilet that morning. You also spend an excessive amount of time praying the dog doesn't have an accident in the middle of the living room carpet while you're at work.

One of the most devastating experiences of the whole house-selling ordeal is the "open house." If your real estate agent suggests such an event, the best course of action is to leave town for the entire weekend. The further away you are, the happier you'll be.

If you are foolhardy enough to stay at home so you can answer questions from prospective buyers, you will be so shocked you may decide to pull your house off the market.

There are three types of people who attend these open houses.

Group 1 consists of the neighbors you don't know. They are just nosy individuals, curious to see the inside of your house.

Group 2 is made up of strangers who are semi-serious about buying a home, buy have no idea what they're looking for. They spend every weekend touring the open house circuit, searching in vain for something to buy.

Group 3 includes people who have nothing to do on Sunday until the doors of the Brown Derby swing open, so they stop at an open house.

All three groups traipse through your home, picking up your Waterford crystal and checking out the crumbs in your kitchen drawers. They feel compelled to evaluate your taste in furniture as too formal, too contemporary, or "interesting."

Sooner or later, someone will come along who isn't shocked by the jelly smears on the refrigerator door, who thinks the carpet is the "perfect" color, and who asks about the property taxes. Instead of seeing the dripping faucets and the hole in the window screen, all they see is their own furniture in the living room.

That's when the sign comes down and you can return to the normal world of finger prints, scattered newspapers, and rings in the bathtub.

But until that day comes, every time you see a "FOR SALE" sign in the front yard, take pity on the hapless individuals inside, knowing that their share of the American dream is just one long anxiety attack.

Mr. Fixit Doesn't Wear A Watch

I have a dream.

One day I will call all the repairmen in town and they will all show up at my door at the same time.

Foolish? Yes, but wouldn't it be a sight to behold!

I sometimes feel I'm destined to spend the rest of my life waiting for the repairman.

Anyone who has wasted an entire day sitting at home waiting for the plumber (who was supposed to arrive at 11 in the morning) knows what I'm talking about.

Think back. When was the last time the electrician or the cable installer or the claims adjustor actually arrived when he told you he would?

I'm sure you've heard the line.

"I'll be at your house at 9:30 tomorrow morning to

repair your dishwasher. Be there."

Big talk from someone who didn't stroll in until just past noon, the very moment eight ladies were sitting down for a little luncheon party. Naturally, they were eating from dirty dishes.

"Make sure you're home between 1 and 2 p.m. Tuesday so our repairman can get inside to fix your refrigerator."

The repairman evidently knew that the melting point for three cartons of ice cream was 3 p.m. That's why he showed up at 4:45.

"Don't worry. The termite inspector will be at your house at 11 a.m. sharp."

By 2 p.m. the termites had eaten away the front door, and when he arrived at 10 a.m. the next day, all that was left was the kitchen sink.

You may think I'm exaggerating. If so, you're probably related to a repairman.

Let's face it. Mr. Fixit doesn't wear a watch. He never knows what time of day it is, so how can we expect him to arrive on time?

I'm fully aware that delays often occur, causing repairmen to be late on their appointed rounds. I know they get stuck in traffic jams. I realize they can't find addresses.

But is it too much trouble to call ahead?

A little message saying you'll be two hours late would be appreciated, guys. Even E.T. had enough sense to phone home.

You see, I'm at your mercy.

When the oven light works but the heating element doesn't, you're the only knight in shining armor I've got. If you can't come and fix the oven, my family is likely to starve.

When the sewer backs up and toilets overflow, you're more valuable than a royal flush.

When the beams turn into sawdust and the roof starts falling down, you're the only one we can turn to for help. Without you, we'll have to resort to a tent.

When I call for help, I'm desperate.

As a naive young bride, the long waits didn't bother me so much. A two-hour delay by the telephone installer just gave me more time to decide whether I wanted a white Princess model or a yellow Trimline phone. Those were the days.

Today, time is a little more precious.

If you say you'll be at my house at 10 a.m., I'm waiting at the front door with a red carpet, a pot of coffee and a smile. But if you don't show up by the time the coffee turns cold, so do I.

By 11 I start to worry. Did I mark the wrong day on my calendar? Did you have an accident? Will the faulty ice maker fill my freezer with little cubes before you arrive to fix it?

By noon, I'm calling your service department, but all I can get is a busy signal. When I do get through, I'm put on hold.

By 3, I'm frantically trying to make arrangements for some other mother to pick up my kids at school.

By 4 I'm searching the kitchen to find something to serve for dinner. I can't risk going to the store. If I miss you, I'll have to go through the whole thing the next day.

By 5 I am muttering obscenities at anyone who talks to me. My mood is vile. I take my frustrations out on everyone.

At 6 my husband opens the freezer and is bombarded

by an avalanche of ice cubes. "I'll fix this thing," he says.

He breaks the water line. Water shoots all over the kitchen. He has to shut off the main valve. I call the plumber. He'll come tomorrow at 10 a.m. Right!

There's just no escaping the wait.

Don't bother trying to convince the repairman that if you have to run out for a little errand, you'll leave the front door unlocked so he can get inside to repair whatever is broken.

"Look, lady, if nobody answers the doorbell, we don't go in," they respond. "You'll just have to schedule another service call."

It took only three days without water to teach me that my life does, in fact, revolve around the repairman's schedule, and not vice versa as we are lead to believe in the TV commercials.

Josephine the Plumber, that wonderfully warm and witty woman who visits any house in distress at a moment's notice, doesn't really exist. She's just a figment of the imagination of some high-priced advertising executive. And I'll lay odds that the ad man's wife is sitting by the phone wondering when the repairman will arrive to fix her washing machine.

I may be getting paranoid, but I suspect the whole thing is part of a plot by the males in our society to keep the woman in the home, "where she belongs."

When you dial the Maytag repairman and you get an answering machine, I think the message is clear. Women in this country are at Mr. Fixit's mercy.

Heigh-ho, Heigh-ho, It's Off To Work I Go

The majority of Americans participating in a recent survey said their job is one of their favorite pastimes. Obviously, the majority of Americans interviewed were not housewives.

In a nationwide survey, "going to work" ranked third in a list of 25 activities, just behind child care and socializing with friends and relatives.

Work beat out such leisure activities as going to the movies, watching television, playing sports, reading, shopping and other categories.

I know this news comes as a big surprise to a lot of our retired residents in Florida who think they're having the time of their lives playing shuffleboard, waxing the car, and visiting the local salad bars. But as a housewife, let me tell you there's a lot of truth to these findings.

Whenever my husband comes home after a "tough" day at the office and collapses into the sofa, too tired to even make a cocktail, I know it's all an act.

"You wouldn't believe my day!" he says with enough anguish in his voice to make me think he just wrestled a dozen alligators in the heat of the summer sun and then went out and built a 20-foot-high cement block wall with his bare hands.

In truth, this man sat in a comfortable chair behind a big desk in an air-conditioned office all day and answered a few phone calls. You call this "tough"? I'd sell my soul to have one of these "tough" jobs that people are always complaining about.

First of all, in the business world there are only adults. No children allowed! That means you never have to worry about taking someone to the potty in the middle of an important phone conversation.

Second, in the business world there are other living people to converse with. You don't have to talk back to the TV set. You don't have to listen to some cemetery plot salesman on the telephone just because he's your only human contact between 8:30 a.m. and 5 p.m. who doesn't drool. At least it doesn't sound like he's drooling.

In the business world you can stand around the water cooler and have deep meaningful conversations about the miniseries that was on TV last night. Or you can sit in the break room enjoying a cup of coffee while some of your fellow workers gossip about some of your other fellow workers.

And best of all, **YOU** don't have to make the coffee! You don't even have to clean up the kitchen. You just call a janitorial-type person and **HE** comes into your workplace and cleans up **YOUR** mess. Talk about pig-heaven!

No wonder millions of women are trading in their diaper bags for briefcases and heading off to job interviews.

Now here's the real kicker. You know all that hard work your husband keeps complaining about when he gets home ... the work that causes him so much distress that he has to take a nap on the sofa because he's too exhausted to do the dishes? Well surprise ... it's not so "tough" after all.

By the time you cut through all that complex business lingo that working people use, you find they're really dealing with simple arithmetic and little projects that require about as much effort as picking up the laundry.

While your husband is solving all those complex little problems at his office, you're stuck in the supermarket with a cart full of groceries, one child who has just pulled the bottom can out of a pyramid of soup cans that is starting to collapse, another child who has emptied the candy shelf and is throwing up on the floor, a gallon of ice cream that is starting to melt, a check that requires two major credit cards, a driver's license and a complete credit history in order to be cashed, while a little old lady with a cane keeps hitting you in the shins. **THIS** is what I call a **PROBLEM**.

Yes, I can understand why most Americans say their job is one of their favorite pastimes.

I can also understand why housework came out on the bottom of the list. I'd trade it for an office job any day!

Packing It In
For Vacation

When Charles Lindbergh made his historic flight across the Atlantic Ocean in 1927, legend has it that he packed only a change of underwear.

Now there's a master in the art of traveling light!

It's also an interesting tidbit to keep in the back of your mind as you pack five suitcases, a wardrobe bag, two overnight bags, three purses, four beach bags, two make-up cases and carry-on baggage for that upcoming week-long family vacation.

If you're one of those people who travel through Europe for three weeks with just two outfits, washing-and-wearing your way through 14 countries carrying only a tote bag and a camera case, you can't appreciate the agony many couples are going through this vacation season.

Even as you read this, some woman in your neighborhood is probably lugging a suitcase down from the attic, fumigating the inside of the luggage, and frantically pulling clothes out of drawers and closets in a desperate attempt to get ready for vacation.

Soon that person will also be pulling hair out of her head as she realizes she's got just three hours to decide what to take, wash all those last-minute choices, fold enough garments to clothe a family of four for a month, and force the items into a suitcase designed to fit under your average size airline seat, which we all know is no bigger than a bread box.

And I'm not talking just clothes. I've got an entire chemistry set for my contact lenses, and it has to go everywhere I go.

Makeup isn't just a tube of lipstick. It's a whole array of paint, powder, gloss, lotion, brushes, mirrors, and little appliances.

And a simple toothbrush isn't sufficient. There's mouthwash to consider. And dental floss. And different brands of toothpaste for each member of the family. I know one family that won't leave home without their water pik.

Even a day trip requires a medicine chest filled with pain relievers, stomach relaxers, bandages, eye drops, and enough medicine to handle any conceivable injury or illness.

The problem with packing is that it requires too many decisions:

"Should I take the hair dryer or the curling iron?"

"How many bottles of tanning lotion will the family consume in two weeks?"

"Should I carry an umbrella or a raincoat?"

"Will the weather be hot or cool?"

"Should I bother packing sweaters?"

"What happens if the kid's only pair of good shoes gets wet?"

The dilemma goes on and on.

And it's not made any easier when the man of the house is hovering over the suitcase making remarks like:

"You're not taking sweaters, are you!"

"Who's gonna drink all that tanning oil?"

"We'll only be gone for two weeks ... we're not moving!"

"This is never gonna fit in the trunk of the car."

This illustrates one of the basic differences between men and women.

The typical male thinks you can pack five days worth of clothes for a 14-day trip. After all, who's going to know you wore the same shirt four days in a row if you're visiting four different cities, unless of course the spaghetti stain didn't wash out.

The typical female, however, knows from birth to pack enough clothes to be ready for any eventuality. Maybe that's why "packing for vacation" tends to be a woman's job.

Take my neighbor, for instance. A recent widower, he decided to take a three-week trip to the Orient. He called

79

his grown daughter at 11 p.m. on the night before he was to depart, asking her to come over and pack his suitcase.

"It'll be fun," he told her. "It'll make you feel like a woman."

She got so mad at the remark that she refused his command.

The next afternoon she got a call from her father during his stopover in Hawaii.

"I forgot my passport," he said frantically. "Could you send it Federal Express?"

A woman's work is never done!

Maybe if Charles Lindbergh had a woman to pack for him, he could have stayed in Paris a few days longer.

The Ding-a-ling Blues

Alexander Graham Bell must not have been a father.

I'd like to think that if he had kids, he never would have invented the telephone.

Five minutes after my daughters were born, their shaky little hands were reaching up toward their ears, grasping at an imaginary telephone receiver.

The first words out of my older daughter's mouth were, "It's for me."

My younger daughter could dial a 1-800 number before she was potty-trained.

But I now realize that the prepuberty phone-a-mania was nothing compared to the teenage telephone trials and tribulations.

It's been years since I've seen either one of my kids without a phone receiver cradled to an ear or a phone cord wrapped around an arm. And it's not a pretty sight!

The phone never rings twice at our house ... at least when the kids are home.

My younger daughter could be in the middle of a shower, but if she hears the jingle of the phone, she can dry off and answer it before I can get up from the sofa.

My older daughter would sell her soul for a car phone, just so she wouldn't miss those important calls.

If the phone call is for either one of my children ... and it always is ... they will go into the bedroom, close the door, stuff a towel in the gap between the floor and the door, and talk into the mouthpiece in hushed tones.

For a parent to overhear even a single sentence would be a fate worse than death.

But if the phone call happens to be for me, as soon as I hang up I face an inquisition.

"Who was that?"

"What did she want?"

"Where was she calling from?"

And on and on and on. But that seldom happens in our house. The bell tolls mostly for my kids.

When the phone does ring for me, it's usually a call I could do without.

"Mom, I missed my ride. Could you pick me up?"

"Mom, I'm at Kathy's house. Could you take us to the movies?"

"Mom, I'm at the mall. Did I get any calls?"

One hot day last summer, my husband spent 30 minutes trying to call home and heard nothing but the busy signal.

"We've got a communications problem," he said at the

dinner table that night. "You kids have taken over the phone and I can't get through to my own line."

The call waiting feature offered by the phone company seemed like the obvious solution. But call waiting didn't turn out to be the boon we thought it would be ... at least for the adults in our house.

Call waiting simply enabled our kids to quadruple the number of incoming phone calls they could take during the average day.

And when they discovered that three-way conversations were possible, a whole new level of communication was achieved. Now my daughter calls two friends, who call two other friends, and before you know it, the entire school is "networking."

About the only way to get my phone back is to buy my kids a separate phone line.

"That's a pretty drastic step," my husband says. "Besides, it might backfire and allow the kids to receive that many more calls."

I guess I just better put up with the "ding-a-ling blues" until my kids leave home and the telephone returns to its rightful owner.

Prom Dress From Hell

If the senior prom isn't over soon, I'm voluntarily committing myself to a mental hospital.

Either that, or you'll find me in the state penitentiary serving an involuntary life sentence for murder.

The victim: my daughter.

The motive: **THE PROM DRESS FROM HELL!**

After nearly $300, more battles than the Civil War, and enough tears to flood Lake Okeechobee, I'm proud to announce that my daughter will be stepping out to her senior prom looking like a stem of broccoli wearing sunglasses.

It all began in February when she announced ... no, make that proclaimed ... that she was going to have a dress made for her senior prom in May.

Furthermore, she would take care of it on her own, thank you, and it had to be done in the next few days. That said, she disappeared.

Had I been June Cleaver, I would have bit my tongue, smiled, told her how wonderful I felt about her learning to take control of situations, and left it at that. But noooooo... I raced down the hall, fast on her heels, trying to fix what I sensed would be a disastrous situation.

"Honey, you don't have to spend your hard-earned money on a prom dress," I told her. "I'll be happy to buy you one. I don't know if the stores are stocking prom dresses this early in the year, but we can go shopping together whenever you want."

"No," she said adamantly. "I've already looked at the stores, and none of the dresses fit me right. I'm shaped like Dolly Parton and the dresses are all made for Twiggy. Sherry's mother knows a dressmaker, and Sherry and her mom are going to help me."

Trying not to show my growing agitation, I counter with "But what's the hurry? You've got three months."

"Sherry's mom says there's a big rush at prom time, and that I'd better do it right now," she said with all the authority an 18-year-old can muster. "I've already ordered the fabric and I've picked out the pattern."

I gulped. "Did you find out how much the material is going to cost before you ordered it?"

"No," she said defiantly.

"Do you have any idea how much it costs to have a dress made? It could be big bucks," I warned.

"No, but Sherry's mother talked to the dressmaker and she said it would be about $60. Anyway it shouldn't matter to you because **I'M** paying for it."

A voice bigger than Martha Rae's is screaming inside my brain: Shut up, shut up, shut up! You can't win! And by the way, who is this Sherry character and why is her mother doing this to me? Maybe I'm jumping the gun. I should probably find out what she had in mind.

"What fabric did you select? A soft pastel? A pretty floral?" I inquired, picturing her waltzing our the front door in a beautiful gown that would make Cinderella envious.

"Oh, Mother, it's beautiful," she said. "It's dark green iridescent taffeta, I think they call it. And the contrasting fabric is going to be black."

That did it! "Don't you think black and green may be a little dark for spring?" I shouted with all the distress of a mother who has failed to pass along the when-to-wear-white rule to her offspring.

"Those colors may be fine for winter, but in the spring and summer people usually wear light, bright colors. You're going to be the only one at the dance dressed like you're on your way to a funeral."

"I don't care," she shouted back. "Besides, Sherry's mother said it would be fine."

As I stomped away, seemingly so did the problem. Months passed. The fabric came in ... even darker than she anticipated ... but she neglected to pick it up from the store. I began to see a glimmer of hope. Maybe Cinderella's gown would fall into place.

But two weeks before the dance I began to panic. Finally I broke down and asked about the dress. She told me she and Sherry had an appointment with the dressmaker, who turns out to live 45 minutes away.

"Take the pattern with you," I told her. "Make sure she thinks it will be flattering. And see what she thinks of the colors. But most important, get a total price before you start the process."

When will I ever learn?

Four hours later she returned without saying a word.

"What did she say about the colors?" I asked.

"She said they'd be OK."

"Did you ask how much she's going to charge?"

"No, but she told Sherry's mother it would be $60 to $80."

I didn't say a word.

When the material cost $40 more than the original estimate, I didn't even utter an "I told you so."

When the seamstress phoned halfway through the project to announce that because it was more difficult than anticipated, the cost would go up accordingly, I maintained silence.

Three days before the dance, when we had to go shopping for shoes, undergarments, stockings and jewelry for the final fitting, I just grabbed my checkbook and we raced to the mall.

But that's when I totally lost control. We agreed on absolutely nothing.

She wanted spike heels, while I tried to persuade her that medium heels for a four-hour dance would be much more comfortable.

The girdle I suggested was "only for old ladies."

And of course all the accessories I recommended were "totally wrong."

She glared. I fumed. And sales clerks, caught in the middle, were obviously ready to pull their hair out.

Tomorrow is the big night. My daughter's dress has a big black bow in the front that looks like a giant pair of sunglasses perched on a stem of broccoli. I swear I'm not exaggerating!

I was lamenting the whole experience with my best friend, who started waxing poetic over her own daughter's senior prom, reliving treasured moments she'd give anything to recapture.

"It was so great," she recalled with melancholy. "I'll truly never forget it."

"No," I replied honestly, "nor will I."

A Toast To Emily Post

Mix together 14 overdressed and under stress teenagers, add several impatient and overworked waiters, toss together with a bunch of gawking diners, and place in one crowded restaurant.

What have you got? Prom night!

May is the month when you catch a glimpse of them in local restaurants. Teenagers, trying to look their best, out for a fancy dinner before their senior prom.

Everyone in the restaurant is dressed in typical going-out-to-dinner-in-Florida clothes: polyester slacks, flats, a leisure suit, maybe a jacket if it's chilly.

And in walks a group of teenagers looking like they just stepped out of an MTV special.

Girls in full-length prom dresses, with hair teased like a wire brush, teetering on heels so high they risk a nose bleed.

Boys in formal attire usually reserved for weddings and costume parties.

Do they look out of place? Yeah!

Do they care? Naah!

This is one of those rites of passage ... a chance for teenagers to pretend they're adults without having adults around to tell them otherwise.

Naturally, I tried to prepare my own teenage daughter for situations such as this.

For the first 18 years of her life I told her how to sit and how to stand. I lectured her about not slurping soup and choosing the right fork to use. I had her practice polite table conversation, and explained why you don't drink out of the finger bowl. I made her memorize the cardinal rule of dinner parties: boy, girl, boy, girl.

And naturally, she resisted even the slightest temptation to put any of my wonderful advice to use. What can I say! When she's at **MY** dinner table, she eats like a pig!

That's why I was really rinsed when I didn't get the opportunity to see my own daughter fumble her way through dinner on her senior prom night. Oh, to be a fly in the soup!

I even joked that I might stop at the restaurant that night. "You wouldn't dare," she glared. So all I got was a second-hand description, but it did my heart good.

"I was so embarrassed," she told me later of her

experience with six other couples at a fancy restaurant before the prom.

"When they looked at the menu, all they could talk about was the prices," she confided. "They kept complaining loudly, 'We should have gone to McDonalds'."

"And every time we went to the rest room, the people at other tables watched us go past like we were a parade or something. They kept staring!

"Sherry was insulted when the waiter tried to put her napkin on her lap, and Tom got mad because the waiter kept filling his water glass.

"Everyone passed around food like we were in a cafeteria. It was humiliating. And they were all asking me which fork to use.

"But the worst was when the bill came. All the boys got up, went to one end of the table, and started arguing and complaining. I wanted to hide under the table.

"They were trying to figure out who ordered what, and the boys were really getting hot!

"My date looked at the bill and said, 'All right, which one of you had the grat-a-tootie?' Nobody knew what he was talking about, so he called the waiter over.

"'Garcon (which he rhymed with harken), there's been a mistake here ... nobody ordered this grat-a-tootie.'

"The waiter looked at the bill, rolled his eyes, and said, 'Monsieur, that is the gratuity. Gratuity is the tip'."

Wouldn't Emily Post be proud!

The Black Hole
Purse-onified

If all the women in America decided to clean out their purses on the same day, the landfills of the world would have to shut down.

All that accumulated trash dumped in one heap would throw Earth off its axis. It would be a global calamity.

My handbag is typical. World War III could start inside my purse and nobody would notice for months.

I don't have any idea how my purse gets so full of junk. It just does.

For a long time I thought it was just my flagrant inability to organize things. Too late in life I learned that nearly every woman alive carries a purse as crammed full as mine. What a relief!

I make it a practice to clean out my purse every Leap Year. That way I don't lose things forever.

Since I'm a born procrastinator, I usually put off the task until late in the year. But recently I accidentally dropped the car keys in my purse (worse than throwing them in the black hole in space) and I was forced to cancel all my weekend plans so I could clean out my purse and rescue the keys.

Here's what I found near the top, where lightweight items sort of float in a state of Limbo:

* Seven gasoline charge receipts, 13 bank deposit slips, a credit slip from Sears, four shredded Kleenex, and my daughter's Brownie membership card dated Sept. 30, 1981.

* A recipe for Thanksgiving turkey scribbled on the

back of a bank deposit slip (I spotted the recipe in a magazine in a doctor's waiting room but never made the turkey).

* A small plastic spoon from an ice cream shop with chocolate chips stuck to it, and a notice written on a scrap of paper reminding me that the Commodore Software Center will host a Users Club meeting June 3 (I'm not quite sure which year).

* Four ticket stubs from the movie theater, two ticket stubs to a charity auction, and one ticket stub that says "admit one" but doesn't explain to what.

* A coupon for mascara "for sensitive eyes" that expired two years ago, and five business cards from my orthopedic surgeon with a note clipped to them that says, "Just want to make sure you never run out!"

* A sheet of paper folded in quarters that has the words "2 AA batteries" written on it, and an unsigned credit card from a now-defunct gasoline company.

There's a second level in every woman's purse that holds heavier objects, the things that are used so frequently they don't have a chance to sink to the bottom. The middle layer of my purse contained the following:

* A comb with 12 broken teeth, a brush that is so tangled with hair that you can hardly see the bristles, a little plastic bottle that used to contain aspirin, and three felt tip pens (all of which are out of ink).

* A book of matches from a fancy restaurant in North Carolina that I ate dinner in three years ago, three tubes of lipstick, several dozen unlucky Lotto tickets, and a free pass from a roller skating rink.

* Five more shredded Kleenex, a pair of sunglasses with one lens missing, and a Band-Aid that looks like it's about 10 years old.

* A scrap of paper containing the name and telephone number of a man I don't even remember. This is the kind of stuff it's best to destroy, because if you have a car accident and the police find the note in your purse, there's no telling what people will think.

* An appointment card for the dentist for June, 1987. (I never kept the appointment, but I kept his name in case I ever got up enough courage to go back.)

The bottom of a woman's purse is where everything heavy ends up. On the bottom of my purse, in between assorted bobby pins and bits of aspirin tablets, I found:

* A 1986 dog tag, a wooden nickel worth one free game of miniature golf, a five-year-old appointment calendar with nothing written in it (but I did have good intentions), and a silver fork I've been planning to give back to my mother since Easter, 1987.

* A package of crackers (actually, a package of cracker crumbs), my contact lens case, a button that says "I HATE MEETINGS," three boxes of matches from various restaurants, and a sea shell.

* The missing lens from my sunglasses, six dimes, 14 pennies, three nickels, and a spray bottle of perfume.

* A little case of Kleenex (empty, of course), three address labels glued to the bottom lining, a cassette tape, the rhinestone Christmas tree pin my daughter gave me four years ago, and three rhinestones.

* More lipstick, two AA batteries, four rubber bands stuck together with a rusty paper clip, and the label from a great bottle of wine (which is so faded you can't quite read the name).

* The warranty for the broken blender that I never took back, a needle stuck through a stick of chewing gum, a burned-out Christmas tree light bulb, and a cracked

mirror.

* Eight expired coupons, five sales receipts, one unfilled prescription, four one-cent stamps, the tops to three pens, a set of chop sticks, and a little plastic sword that once held an olive in a martini.

* One house key, a luggage key, a set of car keys, a key to an unknown lock, and a broken key ring.

Of course every woman knows there are certain things you can't just dump in your purse. So we are also forced to carry around a wallet or clutch purse, containing the items that are essential for survival in the outside world.

And where does this clutch purse belong? Jammed inside the purse, of course.

My clutch purse contains a checkbook, bank deposit slips, hundreds of incomplete check stubs, nine credit cards, check-signing ID cards for every major grocery store chain in Florida, recipes, coupons, and an outdated plastic calendar.

Stuffed inside four cracked and yellowing cellophane windows are class pictures of my daughters from the past four years, my 1965 driver's license, two-thirds of a Social Security card, the business card of an Avon lady from upstate New York, a two-dollar bill, a faded newspaper clipping from 1970 about my sister's wedding, a scrap of paper with the name of a waiter that served us in Disney World, receipts from my entry to the 1988 Publisher's Clearinghouse Sweepstakes, and other assorted treasures.

The change pocket of my clutch purse contains dimes, pennies, quarters, several folded dollar bills, baby teeth, a paper clip, and a lucky penny mounted inside an aluminum horseshoe.

No wonder I never have any money. There's no room!

Don't Improve ... Move

If someone had suggested a year ago that I hire a garbage truck to dump a load of trash in my living room, I would have laughed.

But that's the advice I would give today to anyone even remotely considering a home remodeling project.

With the high cost of housing these days, some of you may be thinking about adding on rather than buying a bigger place.

Don't!

Flip past those newspaper articles under headlines that say "Don't move ... improve."

Resist those do-it-yourself stories in magazines that describe the pleasure you'll get out of turning your hall closet into a powder room for only $250.

Ignore those books you see on supermarket shelves with catchy titles like "If I Had A Hammer, I Could Build My Own Garage."

Better you should pull your toenails out with rusty pliers, get a series of tetanus shots, and sit on a handful of carpet tacks.

Remodeling isn't just a decision to add a few square feet to your home. It's an emotional experience that tests your very existence.

The first shock comes when you start talking cost. No matter how many bids you get, the typical remodeling project will cost more than your grandfather made during his entire lifetime.

The only way to get the cost down is to chuck the wood windows in favor of plastic, go from plasterboard to cardboard, and use your child's old lock-blocks for the outside walls.

After you get through the trauma of signing a remodeling project contract that represents four years of college tuition, two sets of braces and your next three cars, you're ready to begin living in dirt and chaos that would startle even a teenager.

Soon a parade of cement trucks, pickup trucks, panel trucks and vans will drive back and forth through your once-beautiful yard until there is hardly a blade of grass left standing. This "temporary" road will be used daily, leaving ruts so deep a steamroller couldn't level them out.

The trucks carry crews of construction workers, who unfailingly show up at the most embarrassing times. For the next few months you will never be alone!

Once the contractor "breaks through" to your existing house, you are exposed to something more insidious than mold, more annoying than "no-see-ums" and more irritating than sandburs. It's called drywall dust.

For months you will find this fine white powder in your hair, up your nose, down your bra, and under your nails. You have to vacuum your bathtub daily. You question whether the white powder on your morning cereal is really sugar.

The longer the remodeling project goes on, the more you realize that construction is merely a complex matter of scheduling.

The painter can't work until the carpenter is finished. The carpenter can't work until the electrician does the wiring. The electrician can't do anything until the plumber leaves. The plumber can't come until the air conditioning man is through. The air conditioning man can't do his job until the cabinet maker is done. The cabinet

maker can't install the cabinets until the painter is finished. And somehow someone called a "contractor" schedules them all.

After living for a year in the world of pre-hung doors, building permits and tile samples, you begin to wonder if you will ever get back to a normal existence.

Nothing made me appreciate the value of rental property more than undertaking my own remodeling project.

I called a contractor, who walked around the rooms of my house, shaking his head back and forth and scribbling notes on a greasy yellow pad. He measured doorways, thumped walls, and peered at plumbing. He scratched off some paint and peeled away some baseboard.

Then he multiplied some figures in his head and handed me an estimate. An estimate, I later realized, is about as accurate as those race sheets they sell at the dog track.

"How long will it take?" I asked naively.

"Shouldn't take more than two months," he said. "We can start Monday."

LESSON #1: Deal in terms of dates, not days.

Three Mondays later, the contractor showed up at my front door with a crew of workmen who were eying my house like hungry termites eye a new beam.

"These men will take out that front wall," the contractor said. "I'll be back on Wednesday."

The workmen proceeded to demolish the bedroom wall, creating a 12-foot-wide picture window with no glass.

"You shoulda' moved that furniture," a workman advised me as he wrote a message in the dust that now covered my dresser. "It's a real shame about those dents."

LESSON #2: Always be ready for unscheduled demolition.

Tearing down a plaster wall produces the same effect as throwing a dozen bags of flour in the air and whacking them with a baseball bat in front of an electric fan. It gives new meaning to the word "dust."

Just after demolishing the wall, the workmen all headed for the truck and drove away. I figured it was time for lunch. I was wrong. They never came back.

LESSON #3: Don't expect your marriage to outlast a remodeling project.

"How could you let them leave like that?" my husband

screamed that night as he tried to tape sheets of plastic over the missing wall.

"What did you expect me to do?" I shouted back. "Lie down on the street in front of their truck?"

"Why didn't you call the contractor?" he said sarcastically.

"I did. All I got was his answering service."

LESSON #4: Don't sign the contract unless you get the contractor's unlisted mobile phone number ... in blood.

A month later the contractor showed up at my door. He was there, he told me, to inspect the work.

After a quick inspection, he expressed shock and dismay.

"We can't pour the foundation until the plumbing is installed, and we can't install the plumbing until the footers are in, and we can't put the footers in until the inspector comes, and the inspector won't come until ..."

I was obviously distressed.

"But don't worry," he said with a smile. "We'll have this whole project wrapped up in two months. I'll see you on Monday."

Work actually started to progress, which is a good thing. For weeks I had been dressing in the closet, and doing five loads of wash daily.

Plaster dust was everywhere. The dog turned white overnight, every night. Every time I put a magazine down, a small cloud of white dust billowed toward the ceiling. It was not pleasant!

But work was slow, usually accomplished by one workman every other day.

"I'd like to stay longer," the workman would usually say at around 11 a.m., "but I've got to (PICK ONE:

finish another job this afternoon; get new tires for my truck; visit my sick grandmother; or go fishing).

LESSON #5: Try to anticipate this situation by buying a copy of the book "Contractor's List Of Excuses," available at most bookstores.

At some point all work on my project stopped until the building inspector arrived. This moment of anticipation stretched on for days. Then the contractor showed up.

"We could get a lot more work done around here if they came for inspections when they're supposed to," he told me. "Should be about two months after he makes his inspection."

I paid the final draw to the contractor eight months to the date after he first walked through my door.

All the plaster dust is gone. There's a wall between the street and my bed. And I can even laugh about the experience.

But the next time I get the urge to improve, I'm going to pass up the "Do It Yourself" articles and reach for the apartment guide instead.

A State For All Seasons

Lots of people move to Florida and immediately complain about the lack of seasons.

It takes a few years in residence before you realize that Florida does indeed have seasons. They're just a little different.

There's the Tourist Season, when great crowds of pale

people in very big cars drive back and forth on our roads searching for early-bird specials and two-for-one bargains while residents hide in their houses.

There's the Rainy Season, when grass lawns start growing like a venereal disease and residents hide in their houses in fear of being strangled by an out-of-control Floratam runner.

And there's the Hurricane Season, which new residents faithfully observe each year by buying out all the canned goods at the grocery store and then hiding in their houses whenever the weatherman describes a tropical depression in the Lesser Antilles, wherever they are.

After more than a decade in Florida I've discovered another, lesser-known season. I call it Pest Season.

Pest Season starts sometime in May, when the sun begins to heat up the atmosphere to the boiling point, and ends shortly after the summer rainstorms turn the sunshine state into a tropical rain forest.

During Pest Season all sorts of things grow out of control.

While your lawn can be as brown as a desert, little green weeds take root and thrive. Insidious vines race through your grass at five feet per hour, traveling over the fake brick border, across the mandatory hibiscus bushes, and up the side of the house. You can spend days picking the vines out of your yard, and they just grow back stronger and faster.

While weeds threaten the top of your lawn, all sorts of bugs are procreating underneath what residents laughingly refer to as "soil." These creatures thrive on grass roots, and if the bug man is so much as three days late making his rounds, all the fertilizer in the world can't save your lawn.

During Pest Season frogs, snakes, lizards and other creatures that thrive on insects seem to take over the neighborhood. Look out a window at night and you are likely to see a slimy green frog looking back at you, his throat pulsating at the thought of tasty insects.

When Pest Season begins, fruit trees are full of immature fruit and flower bushes are covered with tiny buds. By the time Pest Season ends, the fruit has been ruined by mites, bugs, and insects and usually ends up rotting on the ground. Flower buds are covered with black scale and can only be revived by vast quantities of insecticide.

If you have a pool you can usually detect the onset of Pest Season. It's when the chemical balance of the pool starts going up and down like the Dow Jones average. If you don't dump large amounts of chemicals into the pool on a daily basis, you will end up swimming with green algae, brown algae, black algae, and numerous other life forms you don't even want to think about.

There are other signs of Pest Season. You step on them in the Gulf and get stung by them in your backyard.

So the next time someone steps off the Auto Train and starts complaining about the lack of seasons, hand them a can of insecticide and go hide in your house.

Clothes Encounters

Men and women speak a different language. Nowhere is this more apparent than in the world of shopping.

When a man says he's going "shopping," he means he's going to stop at one store, examine three or four different shirts, and buy the one that most closely resembles the 15 shirts already residing in his closet.

The entire experience will take less than one hour, and that includes driving time to the mall, two minutes looking for a mediocre parking space, and a 15-minute stop at the ice cream shop on the way home.

When a woman says she's going "shopping," she means she's going to visit dozens of stores, look at a wide variety of blouses, examine racks of shoes, and study at least 20 handbags, but she won't find anything that: A.) fits, B.) she likes, or C.) is the right color.

She'll be gone all day, and that includes three hours in the car driving from mall to mall, two hours spent searching for just the right parking places, and four hours trying on things that: A.) don't fit, B.) she doesn't like, or C.) are the wrong color.

In an attempt to help the male readers cut through the

linguistic barriers, I am about to offer a crash course on how to shop for women's clothing. Listen up, men! You'll be glad you did when your sweetheart's next birthday rolls around.

Let's start at the beginning. **FOUNDATIONS** is not the hardware section of the local department store. It is where you buy undergarments. You will not find cement building blocks in "Foundations," and besides, no woman really wants to receive cement building block for her birthday, no matter how attractive the wrapping paper may be.

It might be dangerous to consider a gift of undergarments for a woman unless you are married to her. And if you are married to her, you probably wouldn't consider undergarments anyway. Just the mention of the word "lingerie" makes most men break out into a nervous sweat. So let's move on.

Once you've mastered the "Foundations" mystery, you are ready to tackle **SIZES**. Entire books could be written on the problem of sizes in women's clothing, but I will try to condense the topic in a few simple points.

Consider the categories available: Girls, Toddlers, Pre-Teens, Juniors, Misses, Petites, Ladies, Matrons, Spinsters, Old Maids, etc. The list goes on for miles. I'd like to remind you that class distinctions like these are what brought down the French Empire.

Always remember that "Full-Figured" means "Large," not "Well-Built." And "Better Dresses" means the frock is slightly larger than the cheaper version, so you might get away with a smaller size. Don't ask me why!

This might be the time to point out that all size-10 dresses do not necessarily fit a size-10 female. So if you plan to sneak into your lover's closet at night and copy down the size of her favorite dress, don't count on being able to duplicate it.

The best idea I can suggest is to rise above the rules that govern women's fashion and ask for a receipt. That way she can always exchange the item for something she REALLY likes.

If you ignore this advice and try to discover the logic in women's clothing sizes, you may end up pondering the meaning of life and miss her birthday altogether. This is not good for any marriage.

Above all else, don't ever fall for that famous line, "One size fits all." It never does!

Now a few words about **ACCESSORIES.**

If you're considering giving your spouse a handbag, think big. Those pricey little bags that look so good on a store counter are roomy enough to carry only a handkerchief and a tube of lipstick. Every woman I know would prefer to carry around a suitcase for her belongings.

Jewelry always makes a nice gift. Again, think big! A small perfect diamond can't compare to a large rock that can be flaunted around at the bridge table. After all, observers will be so dazzled by the size that hardly anyone will notice the flaws.

One final piece of advice. When you're buying clothing for the woman you love, don't go cheap and try to pass it off as something expensive. You'll just end up feeling foolish when she returns the merchandise ... and you know she always will!

Taking Stock
Of The Market

I don't usually pay much attention to the stock market.

I know Wall Street is a mysterious force in this country that causes more concern than Ted Kennedy's sex life, but I can't tell you exactly why.

Recently, however, I had some money that had to be invested in something more than a piggy bank, so I started checking out the stock market to find out how it works. You wouldn't believe what I found out.

Let's say that National Widget Co. wants some extra money. You probably think that to get money, National Widget has to sell more widgets at a higher price, right?

Wrong! National Widget simply prints something called "stock certificates" and takes them to a place called "Wall Street" and sells them. Wall Street isn't so much a specific location as it is a state of mind ... and that state of mind is usually panic.

Thousands of stock brokers converge on Wall Street each morning, enter the New York Stock Exchange, and start shouting at each other. Then they go out for an expensive lunch, go back to the stock exchange, shout the rest of the afternoon, pack up their briefcases and get on the train for Connecticut, where they live in expensive mansions. Insiders tell me there's a lot of money to be made in the stock market.

I bet you're asking yourself why these stock brokers would want to pay good money for stock certificates, which are in fact simply pieces of paper.

Well, we're not just dealing with ordinary paper. The

certificates in question have ornate borders in colorful designs, with industrial-type illustrations of oil wells and auto parts and telephone poles, along with financial-sounding words like "debenture" and "aforementioned." That's what makes the pieces of paper so valuable.

So the brokers pay wads of money for these certificates, and the National Widget Co. representatives hurry back to Dubuque with suitcases full of money that can be used for new factories or Lear jets or other executive perks.

Meanwhile, back on Wall Street, the brokers realize they have just paid perfectly good money for perfectly worthless paper, so they try to sell it. Who do they sell it to? Each other!

So all day long they try to con other brokers into buying the stock certificates. This is called "trading." It's sort of like a very long game of Old Maid. Nobody wants to be caught holding the worthless paper at the end of the day.

Naturally, this all makes the brokers very nervous. That's why certain events ... actually almost any event ... can cause Wall Street to panic.

There's even a newspaper devoted to printing news about events that cause Wall Street to panic. It's called "The Wall Street Journal."

Every day "The Wall Street Journal" publishes stories that cause stock prices to plunge or soar.

The Japanese discover that squid causes cancer and prices plunge.

President Bush gets a new set of horseshoes and prices soar. You've probably heard these stories on Dan Rather's news show.

So there you have it. You invest your life savings in the

stock market, and your retirement income pretty much depends on whether George Bush buys new horseshoes.

No wonder they call it a "bull" market!

A Bite Of Paradise

During my years in Florida I've learned to co-exist with fire ants, fleas, mole crickets and palmetto bugs.

And now, in my second decade in paradise, I've become intimately familiar with ... **TERMITES!**

It started in the Spring with a little pile of wings on my windowsill. It ended in a tent, and we're not talking about a camping trip.

Welcome to one more of Florida's little pleasures: termite control.

For years I worried about keeping harmless little ants out of the sugar bowl while termites were secretly gnawing away at the walls of my house. It kind of puts things in perspective.

The problem became noticeable when little black spots suddenly appeared in the wood windowsill in our bedroom.

"Boy is that getting dirty," I said to myself. "I just wiped that off a couple of years ago. I guess I'll have to do it again soon."

Several weeks later the spots looked exactly like egg casings ... those ugly black little rectangles that roaches use to decorate the walls of your house and garage.

"Hmmm," I thought, "I'm going to have to bite the

bullet and call the bug man. These roaches are getting out of control."

But the following day when I opened the curtains, was I in for a shock.

"They must be cleaning house up in heaven today," I screamed to my husband in terror, "because there are at least 50 million wings piled up on our windowsill."

That did it. The exterminator was out the next day with his flashlight and his smelling salts, informing me that we had subterranean termites. As they drilled some holes and forced some goo under the foundation of my house, he mentioned casually: "Don't be surprised if you see some termites in your window for the next few days. They like to come out in the sun to die."

The next day there was nothing. The following day, one or two.

But the third day (and I'm not exaggerating) there were literally thousands of termites having one final fling in my bedroom. They were on the windowsill. And on the floor. Climbing the furniture and heading for the door. There were wings and dead bodies everywhere, but the majority were still partying on the ground and in mid-air.

"Help," I pleaded with my bug man.

"Relax," he shouted back.

My husband and I moved out of our bedroom to give them some privacy, and when we went back three days later, they were goners. That out of the way (and our bank accounts a good bit lighter) we settled back to a typical Florida summer with only killer mosquitoes, giant mutant grasshoppers and no-see-ums to worry about.

But then one fall night it happened. Sawdust started

raining down from the beam in our family room. At first I thought it was my imagination, but then I looked down and saw what looked like an anthill on my green carpet.

Naturally, I did what any sane person would do. I vacuumed the sawdust and hoped the problem would go away. It didn't.

"It's probably something the dog brought it," my husband said.

"I bet it's a packet of seeds that spilled during last year's science project," I said, casting an evil eye toward my daughter.

But when the little anthill got big enough to climb, I knew we had a problem. You don't have to beat me over the head!

A visit from the now ever-so-chummy bug man confirmed my worst fears. This time we were the lucky hosts of dry wood termites.

This time they couldn't just spray or drill under the house. And, since this was a different variety of termite, it naturally wasn't covered under the warranty.

No. For a mere $50,000 cash, my firstborn child, the family jewels and a guarantee of half my husband's paychecks for the next seven years, the exterminators would erect a tent over our house to kill those pesky critters. Of course we would have to pack up half our belongings, the cat, the dog, and the saltwater fish and move out for at least two or three days.

As I sat there shaking, staring at the contract's dotted line, some interesting small print danced before my eyes. Not only was it guaranteed for only one year and not only were they not responsible for any damage done by them or the termites, but I should also not be surprised to suddenly find my house infested with ants, which apparently find dead termites an irresistible delicacy.

The tent is gone. The termites are gone. The ants remain. Where will it all end?

I'm waiting for the day when I awaken to find giant starving anteaters scratching at my doors and licking on the windows, determined to get their dinner! What is this world coming to? If I wanted to live under the big top with sawdust under my feet, I would have joined the circus.

Come to think of it, maybe I did!

A Walk On The Wild Side

Whoever dubbed exercise as "fun" and "exhilarating" has got to be the second biggest liar on the face of the earth.

The first, without a doubt, was my Lamaze coach who euphemistically described labor pains as "a little discomfort." But that's another story.

Today we're discussing those blonde bouncy bunnies with 22-inch waists who bombard you on television with stories extolling the joy and satisfaction of exercise. Give me a break!

During one impulsive period of my life, I started walking five miles a day. I never did experience that new-found energy and that healthy feeling everybody brags about. Walking's not invigorating. It's pure hell!

And it never got any easier.

With blisters on every toe, hair frizzing in every direction, and sweating more water than a fire hydrant, I sulked through town in the dark of night praying nobody saw me.

Neighbors didn't have to water their yard after I passed by. Water poured off my body so fast I was like a walking rain storm. My face was flushed, my clothes were dripping wet, and I huffed and puffed more than the Big Bad Wolf, who, by the way, I felt certain was lurking behind every bush and shadow, ready to pounce. Cursing beneath my breath every step of the way, I waited — breathlessly — for the "fun."

Adding to the misery was the insufferable Florida weather. I started out walking in the evening, but the mosquitoes and the no-see-ums were too much to bear. Next I tried morning jaunts, but between the sun, heat, and traffic, it was more than I could stand. So I settled on getting up before the birds.

First I tried 6 a.m. — not good enough. Then 5 a.m. — better, but that still did not allow enough time for my mandatory morning constitutional. Finally I set the old alarm for 4:30 every morning, but it rarely had a chance to go off. Instead, I would awaken each day between 3 and 4, awaiting the dreaded ring. It was the pits!

Now I don't want all you fitness fanatics on my case about this. I'm apparently not alone in my assessment.

In order to get my mind off my misery, I studied the faces of the other sainted walkers and joggers I encountered on my travels. They grunted. They huffed. And they also frowned as they left trails of sweat behind them. Granted, there were one or two terminally chipper individuals who I'm sure would great you with a bright

smile and a cheery word even from their deathbed. But
mainly these were serious folk who exercised as though
their very lives depended upon it (which, come to think
of it, might be true) and who had obviously been ren-
dered deaf and dumb and were apparently unable to
speak.

"Good morning," said I. "How are you?"

Grunt.

These were not people having "fun."

And the outfits! While I was out there in my size 88
polyester Bermudas and my grease-stained sleeveless
shirt, these folks were parading around in skimpy little
shorts looking like they just ran off the cover of "Health
and Fitness" magazine.

I hated them. The no-bra look was obviously in vogue
for women as they bobbed up and down the road, while
men tended to go topless. And some even glowed in the
dark with reflector tape on their clothes and flashing

lights dangling from their belts.

One day my husband decided he'd get up and join the "fun." Great, I thought. Now he can appreciate what I've been going through.

Wrong! I don't know what I expected from the guy who can wear practically the same size clothes he wore when we met 25 years ago, but a little sweat and pain would have been nice.

But noooooo! Away he went, 20 strides ahead of me, like he was shot out of a cannon. As I raced to catch up with him, gasping for breath, **HE** started giving **ME** a lecture on how to walk.

"Don't pant and gasp like that," he said. "Take long, deep breaths in rhythm with your walking."

Rhythm? This was not an optional move. I was gasping for survival.

Four and a half miles later, I had the shakes, I felt dizzy, and I was on the verge of collapse. My husband? You guessed it. He hadn't even broken into a sweat.

Between that and the day I had an urgent — and I mean urgent — call from Mother Nature at 5:30 a.m., over an hour away from my house and with no relief in sight, I decided to call it quits.

That may make me the only woman left in America who isn't enrolled in some sort of aerobics class. Everywhere I go people are bending and stretching and generally being obnoxiously healthy.

I was window shopping at the mall recently and came upon a vacant store full of women dressed in purple tights gyrating in tune to Richard Simmons. At another mall I was nearly run over by a crowd of exercisers participating in some sort of walk-a-thon.

And you don't go to the hospital these days to visit sick

friends. You go to participate in fitness classes or wellness centers. Baseball is no longer our national pastime. It's been replaced by "fitness."

Personally, I find the whole physical fitness trend about as exciting as cottage cheese.

I realize I'm bucking the trend. All over America people are climbing into sweat suits and rushing off to become physical fitness fanatics.

If you're an up-and-coming young professional in today's society, you've got to play either tennis or racquetball. If you're the wife of an up-and-coming young professional, you've got to spend at least a third of every day hanging out at the courts. (If you think I'm talking about the court house, you're not an up-and-coming young professional, you're a dolt and you don't need to worry about being physically fit.)

Anyway, tennis is a great way to stay fit and at the same time show off those cute little designer outfits that up-and-coming young professionals like to buy. My personal observation, though, is that more than half of the people playing tennis in the hot Florida sun have had a lobotomy, and wear strange-looking headbands in order to conceal the scar.

If you want to sweat in an air conditioned room, aerobics is for you. All you need is some colorful tights, some colorful shorts, a colorful sweat shirt, and a colorful towel to dry off your colorful sweaty face.

They tell me that aerobics isn't exercise, it's fun. After my experience with walking, I'd rather spend the day cleaning the mineral deposits out of my shower heads with a straight pin!

Have Gun, Will Travel

Summer is the time of year when you see lots of newspaper and magazine articles about how to enjoy traveling with your kids.

Whenever I see the words "enjoy" and "kids" in the same sentence, I immediately become suspicious. When the word "travel" is inserted, I'm downright cynical.

Anyone who has ever spent two weeks locked in a tiny car with two youngsters, 25 activity books, a boom box, one set of earphones, and a jumbo package of melted Crayons knows the true meaning of the word "agony."

I'd sooner spend my vacation in Beirut!

First off, a child's body was not designed to sit still for six hours at a time.

The legs were constructed to run and jump, and when they run on the car's ceiling and jump on the back of the front seat, it's a little nerve-wracking.

The arms were formed to toss balls and swing bats. When they toss comic books at the driver's head and swing earphones toward the rear-view mirror, it tends to cause tension.

The mouth was designed to sing, shout and spit, all actions that do not lend themselves to a harmonious situation when three other people share the small interior space of your typical automobile.

And while adults can comprehend (and even cope with) the amount of time it takes to drive nonstop from Florida to the mountains, children only understand time in segments of three minutes. Even if they have their own wristwatch (and haven't tossed it out the window at a passing patrolman) they still will ask that dreaded question, "Are we there yet?" at least 2,968 times during a 300-mile trip.

Kids today have no interest in counting license plates from other states. They couldn't care less about playing the "I Spy" game that kept me occupied when I was a child. Instead, they are filled with remorse about their Nintendo game that is sitting at home, unused.

While reaching your nightly destination gives adults a feeling of accomplishment, it only means one thing to a kid — the return of television.

Vacations should be relaxing. Try relaxing with two children fighting for control of one TV set in a tiny motel room with thin walls and no escape hatch.

Vacations should be educational. Try learning anything in a museum when two kids are scratching their names on a 16th Century skeleton, or running through the halls of an art gallery giggling at the "dirty" paintings.

Vacations should be enjoyable. Have you ever dined out with two kids in a fancy restaurant and had an enjoyable experience?

During the last car trip we took as a family, my husband spent two weeks staring straight ahead, gripping the steering wheel with the same degree of enthusiasm that a drowning man grips a life line.

I spent the same two weeks chewing Valium pills like they were breath mints.

And my two children spent the two weeks staging their own version of World War III.

If the kids had lethal weapons, they would have finished each other off within the first day. I tried to get my husband to stop at a lethal weapons store, but he just drove on, incoherently, as if he had some inner strength, or some inner ear problem and couldn't hear the ruckus in the back seat.

The whole thing was like one of those two-week survival tests.

Traveling with children for a week takes a month of preparation, making sure each child has an equal amount of entertaining travel items. God forbid one child would have six colored marking pens and the other would have only five. Or that they wouldn't be the same colors. Or that one would run out of ink first.

Any of the above situations would cause a skirmish that would send war historians back to their books in amazement.

Let's take tiny toy vehicles, for example. If Child A has a toy car and Child B has a toy truck, Child A won't rest until the toy truck is in his possession. But Child A is not about to give up his toy car in compensation. Thus the two kids squabble like GM and the UAW.

The shrewd mother who wants to retain her sanity buys two toy trucks ... the same model, the same color, the same size, and the same price.

When I was younger and more naive, I used to think that by putting a line of adhesive tape down the middle of the back seat, I could solve the problem of territorial disputes. But after just one trip of hearing, "Mommy, she's got her right toe on my side of the car. Make her get it off!" from the Florida border to the North Carolina state line, I decided to let them slug it out.

Now I'm just happy if they take turns, no matter what they're doing.

If Child A hits Child B in the arm, and Child B kicks Child A in the stomach, as long as they take turns I don't interfere.

If they were firing Scud missiles at each other, I wouldn't mind as long as they were taking turns.

That's an indication of just how desperate I can get on a car trip with children.

I've tried tape recorders and earphones, but it just doesn't work.

"That's no fair!" one child will shout. "She's got my favorite tape and she won't let me listen to it."

"That's because you're wearing my earphones. And now they've got germs, and I can't ever wear them again," the other child will yell.

And pretty soon I'm chewing another Valium and my husband is gripping the steering wheel with new determination.

I guess the only solution is to travel in one of those limousines with the glass window that separates the front seat from the back. As long as the control button is in the front, they can fight it out in the back.

That's as close as I want to get to the battle zone.

The Greenhouse Effect

Don't waste too much time fretting about your overdue Visa bill, or the state of the economy, or the health of your financial institution.

We've got a bigger problem on the horizon.

It's time to worry about something really serious — the earth is getting warmer. That means the polar ice sheets are melting. That means the oceans are rising.

That means Alaska's north slope will soon be part of the Sunbelt.

For people living in Iowa, it's no big deal. But for all of us who have our life savings tied up in a home that's three feet above sea level, we better start investing in water wings. It's time to trade the water beds in for air mattresses.

In case you've been too busy searching for citrus canker on your orange trees and haven't heard the news, scientists have discovered something called the "greenhouse effect," which may make a lot of people in Orlando waterfront property owners in the next few decades.

These scientists claim that all the technological advancements made during this century have changed the atmosphere for the worse. Scientists, by the way, are the people responsible for these advancements, but that's another story.

Usually I don't get too concerned when scientists announce their theories. After all, who really cares if the universe started out as a big bang? Who really understands DNA? Who really knows if the grapefruit diet plan truly works?

But this greenhouse effect has me worried.

I know for a fact that the world is getting warmer. My air conditioning bill is proof positive. This warming trend has a lot of implications.

If I were you, I'd start unloading that beachfront condo now while you still can.

The coastal islands will be just a memory. Sanibel's shells could be washing ashore at the Epcot Center.

Rising water won't be the only problem. The heat will make our present summers seem like a breeze.

The question is, do you really want to stay in what's left of Florida if the temperature is 10 degrees hotter than we already experience?

If you're going to stay, be advised that life won't be pleasant. Say good-bye to that nice green lawn. You might as well build a giant sandbox instead.

You think it's tough to grow tomatoes in Florida now? Just wait!

Don't think you can turn to the air conditioner for solace. You won't be able to afford the monthly bill.

By the year 2100, New York City could have a climate like Daytona Beach. If that happens, Daytona Beach — as well as some parts of Manhattan and most of Florida, would be under water. The "Big Apple" could be the "Wet Noodle." But that's better than being another Atlantis!

Surfers will be riding waves in the Arctic Circle rather than the California beaches. The Beach Boys will be singing the praises of Icelandic girls.

Miami Beach will resemble Venice, Italy, but only the top stories of all those condos will be inhabited. Take an elevator to the first floor and you'll need scuba gear to get out.

What can we do to prepare for this disaster?

Move to Norway, for one.

Or we can petition the government to start building a 15-foot-high seawall around the entire coast. This is an expensive proposition, and it would take some getting used to.

We would have to start thinking of the Gulf as a giant above-ground swimming pool rather than a body of water at our doorstep. And we would also have to take ladders to the beach when we wanted to go swimming.

This greenhouse effect isn't going to be a pretty sight.

That's why I plan to purchase some property in the North Carolina mountains. By the time I'm ready to retire, I figure it will be oceanfront property — the perfect place for my little cottage by the sea.

Serving Wine Before It's Time

It's a proven fact that nine out of ten American men would rather deal with an Internal Revenue Service agent than a snotty wine steward.

I guess there's always the chance that you can bluff your way through an IRS audit. But when you're sitting with your friends at a table in some fancy restaurant and you don't know where to stick the cork just handed to you by the wine steward, there's no way out but to crawl under the table and wait until everyone goes away.

Let's face facts. Hardly anybody can tell the difference between cheap wine that comes in a screw-top bottle and wine that was imported from France 15 years ago, stored at just the right temperature, and sells for $5,000 a bottle.

That's why I buy my wine in the grocery store ... in three-gallon jugs ... made by companies like "The Zucchini Brothers" ... with colorful labels ... from vineyards in Idaho.

But then I'm more comfortable with wine. I don't get

all concerned about drinking white wine with red meat or red wine with fish. As long as it comes in a bottle, I can adjust.

I realize, however, that there are millions of people who spend hours worrying about whether to have the **Frere Jacques '83** or the **Escargot '75** with the baked stuffed cabbage. So I'd like to offer a few tips on how you can bluff your way through any situation and make your friends think you're a wine connoisseur.

First and foremost, always act even more pretentious than the wine steward.

When you're handed the wine list, glance at it briefly, scowl, and say, "Don't you have anything better than this?"

That will catch your server off guard. He'll become nervous. When he does bring you the wine, he will probably be so uptight that he'll spill some on your sleeve. Then he will apologize profusely and tell you the wine is "on the house." Score one for you.

When the wine steward brings the wine to your table, grab the bottle from him and inspect it. Put on your reading glasses. Read the whole label. If it's in French, pretend that you're reading the label. That will really impress your friends. The longer you take reading the label, the more impressed the wine steward will be, too.

This is very important. When the wine steward places the cork in front of you, don't stick it up your nose. And don't reprimand him for dumping his garbage on your table.

Pick up the cork, turn it around in your fingers, and look for any signs of the dreaded wine canker. Smell the cork. Yes, this sounds like a strange thing to do in a fancy restaurant, but those are the rules. If the cork smells strange, lodge a protest and demand a new cork.

If the wine steward pours the wine but neglects to bring you a cork, it means you've ordered a really cheap wine that comes in a bottle with a screw top. In that instance, do not demand to see the cork. You'll only embarrass yourself.

When the server pours a tiny sample of the wine in your glass, don't proclaim in a haughty voice, "I paid for this wine and I want more than that!"

Instead, pick up the wine glass, take a large gulp of wine, swish it around in your mouth, swallow it, and say, "This wine tastes terrible. I demand another bottle."

This will indicate to the wine steward that he is not dealing with any old fool, and that he better come back with the best wine available.

When you finally get a bottle that contains wine you like, hold the glass up in the air, smile smugly, and say something like, "A young wine, but immediately approachable." Everyone at the table will nod in agreement because they don't know any more about wine than you do.

One last bit of advice. If you run up against a really pompous wine steward who makes you feel like some slob who wandered in from the alley, calmly remind the fellow that he has devoted his entire life to serving the ultimate "sole" food, a beverage originally made by peasants who crushed grapes with their feet!

If that doesn't make him "toe the line," he might at least get down from his pedestal and stop being such a heel. If nothing else, it would be a step in the right direction.

How Can You Tell
If It's Winter?

Contrary to popular belief, we do have winters in Florida. If you don't believe me, you must be a tourist. Tourists, you see, refuse to take our winters seriously.

Strike up a conversation about winter with any visitor in January and you'll hear uproarious laughter.

"You call this winter," the tourist will say. "I'll tell you about winter. Why in my home state of (fill in the blank), it's three degrees below zero right now and the wind is whipping snow drifts up to the second story window."

The tourist will then proceed to tell you that winter doesn't exist in Florida, and remind you that you don't know how good you have it.

Well, all you visitors from the North, you may not believe it but we do in fact have a winter season in Florida.

The language we use to describe winter may be a little different from what you're used to hearing from Willard Scott. That's probably why you don't recognize winter when you see it.

"Cold Air Mass," for instance, is a prayer said by Florida retailers who would rather see you in their stores than on the beaches.

"Cabin Fever" is a term we use when traffic gets so bad we don't go out the front door.

"Early Bird Special" is a nifty device we came up with to get traffic off the streets so workers can drive home in the late afternoon.

The "Chill Factor" refers to the temperature of the

water in your swimming pool.

The "Jet Stream" is a weather phenomena that takes place from January through April when dozens of airplanes arrive daily with people seeking a little ray of sunshine.

A "Warm Air Mass" is a special prayer offered by motel owners in mid-January. If the prayer goes unanswered, they get "Frosted."

A "Cold Front" is something you experience by lying face-down on a half-inflated rubber raft in the Gulf of Mexico during the month of February.

"Jack Frost" is a guy you know who lives in a mobile home community. "Frostbite" occurs if the neighborhood dog bites Jack's leg when he goes out to get the paper.

If there's a chill in the air, it's because someone accidentally brushed against the dial on the thermostat, turning the air conditioning system on.

"Shiver" is a word frequently heard at local seafood restaurants, as in "Shiver Me Timbers Fish Special."

"Goose Bumps" refer to those little piles of poop that the neighborhood ducks leave in your backyard.

"Frosty" is a drink you can buy at a fast-food place, and "Bitter" is a word used only to describe chocolate.

"Flurry" is the amount of activity going on at the local shuffleboard tournament, as in "There sure is a flurry of activity at the recreation center tonight."

"Snow" is the white stuff that comes from Colombia and passes through Florida on its way to drug addicts and Yuppies in the rest of the country.

"Snow Storm" is what we say after another day without rain: 'sno storm again today, Ethel.

And if, after all that explanation of language, you still

don't believe we have winter in Florida, go out to the beach and take a gander at the people.

Don't concentrate on the guy in the bright red swim trunks splashing around in the cold Gulf water. He's from Canada. He wouldn't recognize winter in Florida even if he got caught in a freak snow squall.

Instead, take a look at the guy walking along the shore dressed in wool socks, a heavy parka, ear muffs, and corduroy pants. He's a native. He understands winter weather in Florida.

And he knows that sooner or later the weather will warm up, winter will be over, and we can all enjoy spring. Oh, the problems of paradise!

The Joys Of Winter

This may sound like heresy, but I envy the people in Buffalo in February.

They're celebrating winter the way it should be celebrated.

Sky the color of faded blue jeans.

Air so crisp it could injure your lungs.

And temperatures that are cold enough to make Jack Frost's fingers numb.

I love cold weather!

You're probably thinking to yourself, "This woman has been out in the sun too long."

That's just the problem.

After years in the sunshine, I want to experience winter as God intended ... in long johns, a cashmere sweater, and woolen mittens.

I've seen enough flipflops and spandex to last me the rest of my life.

This longing for winter creeps up on me every Halloween. I wait in anticipation, hoping the palm trees will change color. I watch the mold overtake the pumpkin. And I think, "This isn't natural."

By Christmas the winter wanderlust has a full strangle hold. Every time Bing Crosby starts crooning "White Christmas," I cry. During the afternoons I flip the air conditioner to "frostbite," throw a Duraflame log in the fireplace, and cuddle up with the TV watching nature shows about frigid places like Wyoming or Alaska.

By mid-January I'm usually in a full Florida funk, sulking around the house and praying for a sudden cold front.

My kids steer clear. They know I'm likely to unload my last remaining box of winter clothes and force them to model musty coats, wrinkled scarves, and other mysterious items for which there is no apparent purpose.

"Why on earth did you have a fur leg warmer?" my daughter once asked in astonishment, pointing to a muff.

They've never known the joys of hiding those extra pounds you gained during Christmas beneath bulky wool sweaters.

Sure, Florida is great.

But don't you get just a little tired of all these beautiful days?

When your industrial strength deodorant gives out by 2 p.m., don't you suffer just a tinge of regret that you're not dressed in a flannel shirt in 30-degree temperatures?

When you're forced to set your hair twice a day due to the heat and humidity, don't you recall with fondness the times when one trip to the beauty parlor would last an entire week?

When you watch people huddled together at a football game on a blustery Sunday in Pittsburgh, don't you feel even a hint of envy?

Or how about those bracing walks in the snow? Under a bright winter moon? Followed by a cup of steaming cocoa?

OK, so I'm getting a little carried away.

It's hard to sell the joys of cold weather to a bunch of people who have had their snow shovels bronzed.

I'll just have to plead my case with the people from Buffalo ... in person. They'll be here in February, celebrating winter the way it should be celebrated ... in Florida!